THE INGENIOUS
LANGUAGE

Andrea Marcolongo

THE INGENIOUS LANGUAGE
Nine Epic Reasons to Love Greek

*Translated from the Italian
by Will Schutt*

Europa
editions

Europa Editions
214 West 29th Street
New York, N.Y. 10001
www.europaeditions.com
info@europaeditions.com

*This book has been translated with generous support from the Italian
Ministry of Foreign Affairs and International Cooperation.*
*Questo libro è stato tradotto grazie a un contributo per la traduzione
assegnato dal Ministero degli Affari Esteri e della Cooperazione
Internazionale italiano.*

Translation by Will Schutt
Original title: *La lingua geniale. 9 ragioni per amare il greco*
Translation copyright © 2019 by Europa Editions

Library of Congress Cataloging in Publication Data is available
ISBN 978-1-60945-545-3

Marcolongo, Andrea
The Ingenious Language

Book design and cover illustration by Emanuele Ragnisco
www.mekkanografici.com

Prepress by Grafica Punto Print – Rome

Printed in the USA

CONTENTS

For Livorno,
for Sarajevo,
for me

y

INTRODUCTION

> The sea burns the masks;
> the salt sets them on fire.
> Men and all their masks
> blaze up on the shore.
>
> You alone will outlive
> the conflagration of Carnival.
> You alone, unmasked, conceal
> the art by which we live.
> —GIORGIO CAPRONI, from *Chronicle*

It is "strange"—very strange—writes Virginia Woolf, "that we should wish to know Greek, try to know Greek, feel for ever drawn back to Greek, and be for ever making up some notion of the meaning of Greek, though from what incongruous odds and ends, with what slight resemblance to the real meaning of Greek, who shall say." Strange because "in our ignorance we should be at the bottom of any class of schoolboys, since we do not know how the words sounded, or where precisely we ought to laugh."[1]

I'm strange too—very strange.

And I'm grateful for that strangeness, which has led me

[1] Virginia Woolf, *The Common Reader*, "On not Knowing Greek!" (New York, NY: Harcourt, Brace, 1948)

to write this book about ancient Greek, having had no plan to—and no plan is always the best plan. I pushed myself not only to increase my knowledge of Greek, but also to talk about it.

To you. From the bottom of the class (naturally) to this; but at least now I have an idea about where precisely we ought to laugh.

Dead language and living language.

Bane of high-school students and adventures of Ulysses.

Translation and hieroglyph.

Comedy and tragedy.

Understanding and misunderstanding.

Most of all, love and hate.

Revolt, then.

Coming to understand Greek is like learning how to live your life: not a question of talent but of determination.

I have written these pages because I fell in love with Greek when I was a young girl. That makes it the longest romance of my life, when all is said and done.

Now that I am a grown woman, I would like to try to kindle (or rekindle) the romance in those who fell out of love with it, in all those who encountered this language *for adults* when they were *just kids* in a classroom. I'd even like to make sparks fly in those who have no previous knowledge of the language.

This book is about love: love for a language and, more importantly, for the human beings who speak it. Or, if no one speaks it anymore, for those who study it either because they are forced to or because they find themselves irresistibly drawn to it.

It does not matter if you know ancient Greek or not. There are no exams or pop quizzes attached to this book, though there are surprises. Loads of them.

Nor does it matter whether you studied the classics in school. All the better if you didn't. Should I succeed in guiding you through the labyrinth of Greek on the wings of my imagination, you'll arrive at the end of this journey with new ways of thinking about the world and your life—whatever language you use to articulate them.

If you did study it, even better. Should I manage to answer the questions you've never asked or that you never had answered, maybe when you're done reading this you'll have recovered parts of yourself that you lost growing up and studying Greek without really understanding *why*, and maybe those parts will turn out to be useful to you now.

In either case, these pages are a way for you and me to take a crack at thinking in ancient Greek.

Over the course of our lives, all of us encounter Greek and the Greeks at one time or another. Some of us with our legs tucked under a school desk, others while watching a tragedy or comedy unfold at the theater, others still in the cool white corridors of the world's many museums—in each case, what it actually meant to be Greek is no more vivid and alive to us than a marble statue.

Sooner or later, each one of us is told, "Everything beautiful and unparalleled that has been said or done in the world was said or done by the ancient Greeks first." And, therefore, said or done in ancient Greek. Told may be the wrong word, since, at least if you grew up anywhere in Europe, for more than two millennia this idea has been embedded under our skin and in our minds.

Almost no one has direct knowledge of ancient Greek; the one thing we can be certain of is that there are no more ancient Greeks who speak ancient Greek. We have only heard that it was spoken and never heard the language itself. That's how things have stood for centuries.

Meaning, this apparent Greek cultural inheritance has been generously handed down to us by an ancient race that we don't understand in an ancient language we don't understand.

How extraordinary.

It is terrible to be told you must love a subject that you don't understand; you immediately hate the subject.

The sight of the Parthenon marbles or the Greek Theater of Syracuse fills us with pride, as if these ancient Greek relics were the work of our ancestors, of our distant great-great-great grandparents. We like to imagine them under the sun on some island, busy inventing philosophy or history, or attending a tragedy or comedy at a theater on the side of a hill, or admiring the starry sky at night and discovering science and astronomy.

Yet deep down we always feel like we're on shaky ground, as if we were being tested on something quite foreign to us, as if we had forgotten some important chapter on ancient Greece. And that chapter that now seems foreign to us is the Greek language.

"A Greek," writes Nikos Dimou in all his unhappy glory, "a strange, absurd, tragic moment in the history of humanity."

Not only do we approach our ancient Greek cultural inheritance as a dispossessed, ill-equipped people, but if we try to claim a shred of what "Greekness" has handed down to us, we become victims of a backwards and obtuse education system (in my "bottom of the class" opinion, which, after this book, might earn me an F and expulsion).

The classics, at least as they're taught in Italy, appear to have no other goal than to keep the Greeks and their Greek as inaccessible as possible, high up on Olympus, mute, glorious, and clouded by a reverential awe that often turns into divine terror and very earthly desperation.

Current teaching methods, with the exception of those practiced by a handful of enlightened teachers, guarantee that anyone who dares to approach Greek will hate the language rather than love it. The result is total surrender before a heritage that we no longer want to know, because as soon as we bump up against it, our confusion has us running for our lives. Most of us set fire to the ships behind us as soon as we've fulfilled our course requirements.

Many readers will shudder to recall their fear and exertion, their anger and frustration with ancient Greek, and recognize their own struggles in mine. Yet this book was written with the conviction that it makes no sense to know something that you don't remember, especially after five-plus years of sweat and tears.

This book is not, therefore, your conventional guide to ancient Greek. It is neither descriptive nor prescriptive. It makes no claims to be academic (that breed of book has been around for millennia).

Sure, it does demand passion and a willingness to be

challenged. It's a literary (not literal) tale about a few particular aspects of the magnificent and elegant ancient Greek language—its concise, explosive, ironic, open-ended modes of expression, which—let's be honest—we unconsciously pine for.

Whatever you've been told (and more importantly not told), ancient Greek is first and foremost a language.

Every language, and every word of that language, functions to paint a world. And that world is your own. It is thanks to language that you can formulate an idea, give voice to a feeling, communicate how you're doing, express a desire, listen to a song, write a poem.

In an age where we're all connected to some*thing* and almost never to some*one*, where words have given way to emojis and other modern-day pictograms, in this increasingly precipitous world where reality is so virtual that we now broadcast our daily lives as we live them, we no longer understand one another, not in deed and not in word.

Language, or what's left of it, is becoming boring. How many of you have placed a call today, I mean actually dialed a number to hear a human voice, for love? When was the last time you wrote a letter, I mean actually put pen to paper and licked a stamp?

With every hour, the gulf between the meaning of a word and how it is interpreted grows in direct proportion to our regrets and failures, as do our misunderstandings and silences. We are slowly losing the ability to speak a language—any language. The ability to understand and make ourselves understood. To put complex things into plain, honest, simple words. Abilities ancient Greek had in spades.

It might seem strange (I said at the outset I was strange) but reading this book about Greek could come in handy for your daily lives (and not just on the occasion of some long overdue class assignment; leave it to life to take care of that). Yes, I mean *that* ancient Greek. Approached fearlessly (and with a healthy dose of folly), Greek looks you in the eye and continues to speak to you. Loud and clear. So that you can think and therefore utter a desire, a sound, declare your love or loneliness; so that you can finally take back your world and put it into your own words. Because, to quote Virginia Woolf again, "it is to the Greeks that we turn when we are sick of the vagueness, of the confusion . . . of our own age."

Writing this book about ancient Greek was an extraordinary experience for me, akin to rediscovering the meaning of some Greek words inscribed on a tablet a thousand years ago and immediately erased at the end of the lesson—forgotten.

I started out with a memory of myself when I was a child slogging through an alphabet different from my own, and wound up looking at the language, and therefore at human nature, completely afresh.

I recovered books from boxes that had survived over ten moves, books from when I was fourteen, books in which I had written the names of my classmates next to the lists of declensions. I also recovered the college textbooks that have followed me from one life to the next, one city to the next, more than the keys to all the houses I have lived in and left behind.

I tried to banish the thoughts that had tormented me for over a decade, and I discovered all it took was sharing them with my friends: they, too, were leaving behind the same thoughts, and most of the time they were unaware that they were doing so. We'd never told each other about them.

I set out to help kids still grappling with high-school Greek today only to end up learning from them. The questions they asked me are the same I used to ask myself when I was struggling with Greek and failing at life. Once the question's asked, it's impossible to rein in our curiosity as long as we don't give up; I didn't give up, though it took a long time to find or imagine the answer.

I laughed with many friends, now adults, who went through the same misadventures when they were struggling with ancient Greek, and I discovered that anyone who has come across this language has a trove of embarrassing stories buried in their closet. (Cue laughter.)

Most of all, I tried to describe the quirks of ancient Greek for those who had never studied it. Incredibly, those people understood me. We understood each other. Well. Or at least, maybe, better than before.

Thanks to aspect in the Greek language, I, who am very strange, learned to look at time in another way and then to talk about.

Making wishes in the optative and calculating how willing I was to make them come true, I blew on so many dandelions that nowadays they're hard to find in the fields of Sarajevo, where I live, at the end of spring.

To the dual, a number in the Greek tongue that means we two—and only we two—I said, I love you.

I realized how cruel the silence between us and the Greeks is, but I also learned that certain music is better seen than heard.

I even made peace with my name, Andrea—a boy's name in Italian—a cause I thought lost.

Writing this book, "the strangeness in my mind," to borrow Wordsworth's phrase, became paradoxically less strange. In short, thanks to ancient Greek—understanding it or at least intuiting it—I succeeded in saying more, rather than less, to others and to myself.

I hope that the same happens to you as you read these pages, and that you will arrive at the end knowing when to laugh and how to relish ancient Greek, at least once in your life.

THE INGENIOUS LANGUAGE

WHENEVER: ASPECT

Time present and time past
Are both perhaps present in time future,
And time future contained in time past.
If all time is eternally present
All time is unredeemable . . .

Footfalls echo in the memory
Down the passage which we did not take
Towards the door we never opened
Into the rose garden . . .
—T.S. ELIOT, "Burnt Norton" from *Four Quartets*

Time, our prison. Past, present, future. Late, soon, yesterday, today, tomorrow. Always. Never.

Ancient Greek paid time little mind. The Greeks expressed themselves in a way that took into consideration how actions affected speakers. Free, they always asked themselves *how*. Imprisoned, we always ask ourselves *when*.

Not the lateness or earliness of things but how things take place. Not the moment things take place but how things unfold.

Not tense but aspect. Aspect is a category of ancient Greek that refers to the quality of an action without situating that action in the past, present, or future. Ants that we are, we tend to arrange what happens along an exact timeline, and everyone has one, be it straight or zigzag.

Events were seen in their concrete becoming, and tense arrived later, with other secondary, linguistic categories. If it ever arrived; sometimes, many times, the "time of things" never turned up at all.

In lines 37e to 38c of the *Timaeus*, in order to talk about time, Plato employs every aspect of the verbs γίγνομαι, "to become," and εἰμί, "to be":

Ἡμέρας γὰρ καὶ νύκτας καὶ μῆνας καὶ ἐνιαυτούς, οὐκ **ὄντας** (present) πρὶν οὐρανὸν **γενέσθαι** (aorist) τότε ἅμα ἐκείνῳ συνισταμένῳ τὴν γένεσιν αὐτῶν μηχανᾶται· ταῦτα δὲ πάντα μέρη χρόνου, καὶ τό τ᾽ **ἦν**(imperfect) τό τ᾽ **ἔσται** (future) χρόνου **γεγονότα** (perfect) εἴδη, ἃ δὴ φέροντες λανθάνομεν ἐπὶ τὴν ἀίδιον οὐσίαν οὐκ ὀρθῶς. λέγομεν γὰρ δὴ ὡς **ἦν** (imperfect) **ἔστιν** (present) τε καὶ **ἔσται** (future) τῇ δὲ τὸ **ἔστιν** (present) μόνον κατὰ τὸν ἀληθῆ λόγον προσήκει, τὸ δὲ **ἦν** (imperfect) τό τ᾽ **ἔσται** (future) περὶ τὴν ἐν χρόνῳ γένεσιν ἰοῦσαν πρέπει λέγεσθαι.

For simultaneously with the construction of the Heaven He contrived the production of days and nights and months and years, which existed not before the Heaven came into being. And these are all portions of Time; even as "Was" and "Shall be" are generated forms of Time, although we apply them wrongly, without noticing, to Eternal Being.[2]

[2] Plato, *Timaeus*, trans. R. G. Bury, Loeb Classical Library 234 (Cambridge, MA: Harvard University Press, 1929).

Τό τε **γεγονὸς** (perfect) εἶναι **γεγονὸς** (perfect) καὶ τὸ **γιγνόμενον** (present) εἶναι **γιγνόμενον** (present), ἔτι τε τὸ **γενησόμενον** εἶναι (future) **γενησόμενον** (future) καὶ τὸ **μὴ ὂν** (present) μὴ ὂν (present) **εἶναι** (present), ὧν οὐδὲν ἀκριβὲς λέγομεν.

And besides these we make use of the following expressions,—that what is become is become, and what is becoming is becoming, and what is about to become *is* about to become, and what is non-existent *is* non-existent; but none of these expressions is accurate.[3]

More than anything, aspect was a manner of dividing human and world events into two categories, complete and incomplete—*perfective* and *imperfective*. Or rather, beginning and end. Every language puts forward a particular vision of reality. If tense is merely secondary in ancient Greek, then there exist a beginning and end to things. Of every thing.

In Greek, aspect indicated the duration of every beginning and every end. The length and manner of an action. How it began, how it unfolded, how it ended. What it became. Aspect, in particular, helped express what is born of every beginning and every end, and how it is born.

What happens if you saw and now know, if you trusted and now believe, if you wrote and now the blank page is filled with words. If you left and if you arrived. When doesn't matter—now you're here.

It's hard for us to wrap our heads around, since we

[3] Ibid.

came into the world believing every beginning and every end exist in time, that there's either too much of it or too little, and what time there is is all we have. It's hard for us to make out, since we speak and think in a language in which, as is the case with most modern languages, every action is attached to a specific moment in time—to the past, the present, the future—and yet nothing can be fixed in time, because time will always change into something else. Has, in fact, already changed. It's hard for us to really notice when something has occurred, since we trust that time will heal our every wound. It's hard for us to think outside of time, but time doesn't exist; there exists an end to all beginnings and a beginning to all ends. Farmers and sailors know this: Farmers reap only to sow and reap again. Sailors dock only to raise anchor, cross the sea and dock again. Because we're always eyeing the clock, the planner, the calendar, and organizing our lives around time, it's hard for us to see that everything changes and everything stays the same. "I'm staying" and "I'm waiting for you" share the same root in the Greek verbs μένω and μίμνω.

It's hard for us but wasn't for those who spoke ancient Greek, a language that perceives process rather than time and expresses with the aspect of verbs the quality of those things that always appear to pass us by, since we're always asking *when* and never intuiting *how*.

Greek verbal aspect may be one of the most glorious legacies of Proto-Indo-European, one of the first (now vanished and therefore hypothetical) languages spoken on earth.

The languages that came after did nothing but squander the intellectual and linguistic stores of Proto-Indo-European in the name of economizing. *The economy principle*—that's exactly how linguists refer to the simplification and trivialization of language.

Over thousands of years, as societies transformed, populations moved, and nomads became shepherds who later became city-dwellers, you needed to express yourself quickly, make yourself understood, and understand. Paradoxically, as the world grew more complex, a simpler language was called for. Which is exactly what happens when reality becomes hard to express. Look at our current mode of communication: emoticons are our modern pictograms, no one knows how to use the phone, and we are forgetting how to speak.

Proto-Indo-European envisioned a completely original verbal system. It didn't propose a regular pattern of conjugation based on time, like the one we're used to and that we learn in elementary school ("I eat," "I was eating," "I have eaten," "I ate"). Instead it proposed independent verb stems completely detached from time.

Starting with Homer, ancient Greek chose to adhere to Indo-European originality and its pure and ancient way of regarding the world outside of time.

As I was saying, it's hard for us to leave behind the *when* of things and concentrate on the *how*. Hard because we're now in a linguistic rut and don't know how to speak without time.

Let's take a look so that we might learn. Let's try to understand aspect, so we can speak it. Because time has no words, but aspect does. We can—we always must—find the words.

For those who haven't studied Greek, trying to understand aspect will be an exercise in linguistic freedom. For those who have studied Greek in high school or college, it might be like getting answers to questions that never got asked. More than an exercise in linguistic freedom, it may be linguistic freedom itself. For some, a revolution. For everyone, payback for all those years spent memorizing verbs you didn't know the meaning of.

In today's textbooks, Greek aspect occupies an average of zero to a half page, while verb charts occupy an average of about a hundred.

I'm well aware that learning a foreign language—dead or alive, that's what Greek is—takes practice, dedication, and perseverance. A lot of memory is required to remember that which isn't *linguistically* ours. (Is learning Japanese all that different?) However, if you don't comprehend the meaning of the language as a whole, that effort is an end in itself—and culminates in little more than a class quiz. Without meaning, we're left with incomprehension: of the language that we're studying and more importantly of the reason we're studying it.

If you studied Greek, you may not remember a word of it today, but you'll definitely remember afternoons spent repeating one paradigm after another. That's what happens when we don't get the point of what we're memorizing. That's what happens when we apply our own—temporal—linguistic categories to languages devoid of them: forced oblivion. Nothing survives but the memory of a spring afternoon slogging through a subject you planned to forget as soon as possible; for most people, forgetting begins the minute they've finished their final exam.

I'll attempt to explain aspect by recalling my own adolescence ticking off paradigms from memory. I recited them religiously without a whit of understanding. I may as well have been reciting Vedic verses, Buddhist mantras, Surahs from the Quran. Even today, as soon as I hear "φέρω" I respond, Pavlovian-like, "οἴσω." In class, I would transcribe verbs on the page by making marks (and crossing my fingers), and my understanding of the language stopped there.

I am neither the first person nor the last. In fact, I know the same thing is going on right now, in hundreds of classrooms, to students born in the year 2000 (AD), students who learned to use a cell phone before a ballpoint pen.

So, I will primarily try to address those currently in the grip of youth, those who in 2019 are probably a bit burnt out in high school or college, to give a little meaning to their afternoons and their all-nighters. Trust me, what you're learning has meaning, beautiful meaning, even if it took me fifteen years and a Classics degree to get it.

Mulish me!

Let's begin with a story.

487 BC. Wee hours of the night in one of the shadiest bars in Piraeus. Cloudy sky, the sound of waves lapping against the triremes tethered to the port, a handful of lanterns lit. Waxing moon.

Tonight, two friends have had a few too many. One has women troubles, the other's merch didn't make it to Halicarnassus. They're considering paying a visit to the oracle of Delphi tomorrow to seek advice. Their mood is pitch black.

They go back and forth on the subject until they're smashed on the strong Greek wine that the Greeks water down.

Maybe our friends haven't watered it down enough. Tonight is one of those nights you need a pick-me-up. (We've all been there.) As in life, so in the tavern: in the end, the bill arrives, and it's steep. Our friends could be gentlemen, pay up, and exit with their heads held high, but instead they get the notion to skip out on the bill. Of course, they're so drunk that the innkeeper will catch them before they've rounded the corner. But they decide to make an escape anyway, and in ancient Greek the word for "escape" is φεύγειν.

Now, in order to understand which aspect to use, we need to put ourselves in the shoes, wallet, and, above all, Greek language of the innkeeper.

The innkeeper can express his displeasure in just three aspects by fishing up—carefully, by no means at random—one of the three stems (this is what I was referring to earlier when I spoke about our Indo-European heritage) of the verb φεύγειν:

1. **Φεύγουσιν, present aspect or stem**: "By Zeus! Check these two out, they're running away!"

There's our innkeeper leaning against the black cask when he sees our two friends making their escape. One trips on the steps, the other loses a shoe. In short, this pitiful sight is taking place right before his eyes—and our heroes probably won't get far.

2. **Ἔφυγον, aorist aspect or stem**: "By Zeus! These two creeps better not be thinking about running away."

There's the innkeeper sitting on his barstool. He can't wait to close the joint, tomorrow he has to get up early, his wife will be moaning and groaning as usual, etc., and as this cocktail of thoughts is swirling in his head, it occurs to him that these two guys are going to stiff him.

It doesn't matter whether he witnesses the scene or not (he may be dead tired, his eyes at half-mast), the point is that the act of running away is a foregone conclusion and there's no reference to duration.

3. **Πεφεύγασιν, perfect aspect or stem**: "May Zeus strike these two bastards with lightning, they ran away!"

Cooked after a long day's work, the poor innkeeper can't believe his eyes: before him materializes a table full of empties—one cup's even chipped—the bill wafting in the mistral, and no trace of our two friends.

The two men escaped a while ago, and the innkeeper is left to pick up the pieces.

Let's leave our two drunk (and fictional) friends to their fate and return to the (true) story of the language and *its* fate.

First, aspect was a precise grammatical category of ancient Greek, as respectable as any mood, person, tense, or voice that we use today to perform the primary function of language: to understand one another and make ourselves understood.

Greek Wine

I couldn't call myself a *Chiantigiana* if I didn't take a moment to talk about ancient Greek wine.

Variously called the nectar of the gods, Dionysus' blood, or Olympian ambrosia, wine used to have a high alcohol content due to Greece's scorching heat and the custom of harvesting grapes late, after the leaves on the vines had fallen.

Consumption of the drink dates back to the Mycenaeans, around the end of the second millennium BC, as findings of drinking cups show and chemical tests have confirmed.

Viticulture was practiced throughout Greece, and the *oikistes* in charge of establishing colonies overseas for the motherland and exporting the customs and manners of the Greeks throughout the Mediterranean would load their ships with grape shoots to be planted in terra nova. That is how viticulture reached the coasts of Africa, Southern France, Spain, and Italy. The last was sometimes called Enotria, or "the Land of Vines," on account of the excellent wine produced in the region.

Earlier we mentioned that the drink was diluted, not only to keep order, obviously, but primarily as a matter of identity: the Hellenes recoiled at the sight of "barbarians" drinking pure wine. In Book 12 of the *Iliad*, Nestor offers the physician Machaon "Pramnian wine" (i.e., wine from Ikaria, considered the first DOC wine in history) mixed with white

The mystery is why a category as fundamental as this is now treated like an extravagance, a pointless option.

One definition of the value of aspect goes like this: aspect indicated not only the quality of an action but the manner in which it occurred and how the speaker felt about it.

As you may have noticed, I slipped into the past tense while defining aspect, because this grammatical category, this way of evaluating the quality of events and their flour and grated cheese. Pramnian wine was a delicacy; the Homeric heroes really did use this concoction to treat wounds or lift their spirits after a long-drawn-out battle. The mash had a name; it was called kykeon, κυκεών.

For the Greeks, the symposium (meaning "drinking together") was the optimal occasion for consuming wine: not only did it serve a recreational function, but it was demanded during moments of civil, intellectual, and political debate. While participants ate and drank, stretched out on *triclinia*, the poets and *aoidoi* sang about Greece's shared history, beginning with the poems of Homer, to bolster their sense of belonging to a community. It was the duty of the head of the symposium, the symposiarch, to establish how much wine to consume and how to dilute it. Wine glasses came in a variety of shapes with different names. The most important vessel was called a krater and was used to serve both water and wine.

Drunkenness had a religious, almost mystical valence. In fact, the Greeks believed that by enabling men to let down their guard, intoxication helped them approach divinity. That's where we get the famous saying "ἐν οἴνῳ ἀλήθεια," *in vino veritas*, coined by the poet Alcaeus and used to this day to justify far less spiritual benders.

Finally, wines were deliciously classified by their color (white, black, mahogany) and aroma (rose, violet, resin).

consequences rather than by nailing events to the wall like wedding pictures in a present-past-future schema; in short, this question of *how* in ancient Greek has been lost to us forever. Even my computer's autocorrect doesn't recognize the word "aspectual." "Wrong!" it keeps telling me as I write, underlining it red—forgotten.

Sure, in my native Italian, we almost unconsciously

resort to various circumlocutions to indicate whether an action is short-lived or occurred at an exact time. But we don't get the value of Greek aspect anymore, because for over a couple millennia our "linguistic sentiment"—our way of seeing the world and putting it into words—has gone without. Worse: we've lost it forever, it's fallen through a hole in our pocket.

Maybe someone gets it in Hawaii, where they speak one of the few languages in the world in which aspect has survived (sticking it out, admittedly, amid those endless words linked by the letter *u*). Even Serbo-Croatian (a language distinct from Serbian, Croatian, Bosnian, and Montenegrin ever since the war waged for political rather than human ends) divides verbs into perfect or durative according to aspect. We, who have disowned our Indo-European roots, must use our imaginations and struggle to understand it.

Before things get complicated, let's quickly recap:

• **present aspect**: the action is durative, happening at the moment. It can be represented by a straight line followed by an ellipsis that stretches on to infinity:

———————————— ....

Example: καλέω, "I'm calling you." Out of my mouth spill the letters that spell your name—à la *Lo-li-ta*, to drag Nabokov onto the dance floor.

• **aorist aspect**: the action is momentary, taken for what it is. It can be represented by a nice fat dot.

Example: ἐκάλεσα expresses *the idea* of calling you. When, why, and how don't matter.

'Εκάλεσα can correspond to the simple past only in the indicative mode. In all other cases, the generic "I'll call you," with no other reference to when or where, vaguely renders the idea. It's the kind of thing you hear after certain dates.

• **perfect aspect**: the action is completed, there's no chance of appeal, and all that you're left with are the consequences. It can be represented by a circle:

◯

Example: κέκληκα, "I called you" and now I'm pulling my hair out because you didn't call back—the date was a flop, I fear.

So fundamental for Greek speakers was the aspectual value of an action that it handily defeated the temporal value of the same action. Indeed, time was only alluded to by the indicative mood and expressed through add-ons, like prefixes and suffixes, while for every other mood (the infinitive, subjunctive, optative, participle, and imperative), aspect is what made all the difference. Once again: not when but how.

When—never.

The time has come to take a close look at (and imagine to ourselves) this manner of making oneself understood. In order to do that, we need to look at the stems mentioned earlier, our glorious and squandered Indo-European inheritance. This is the underlying reason why students are taught to memorize paradigms. The *core* reason.

The stem is the part of a word that remains unchanged no matter how the verb is inflected, and, although the difference between "stem" and "root" in English is of less importance than it is in many languages that are more highly inflected (for example, Latinate languages like Italian), this definition holds also for English. The stem is what's left when all inflections are removed—the root what remains when all affixes are removed, a form that can no longer be analyzed, is irreducible.

Ancient Greek came out of the Greek Dark Ages bearing three distinct stems for every verb, like souvenirs: three stems connected to aspect—present, aorist, perfect—in addition to the future (which we'll get to later) and passive aorist (little more than a sub-group of active aorist).

Multiply everything by five and those who still remember their classics education will realize why you had to recite those paradigms as if they were the Lord's Prayer. (That's exactly what I was told: "You need to know these paradigms as well as you know the Lord's Prayer.") You were learning all five stems of the same verb. In other words, your teachers were reconfirming the fact that you didn't get the language and therefore had to learn it by rote. By rote! That is, the quickest way to forget.

But the ancient Greeks got stems at a glance, so well that they knew the same verb contained distinct parts and may have suspected those parts were connected.

The Greek Dark Ages

Many people have attempted the titanic undertaking of shedding light on the Greek Dark Ages, and none has come out of that darkness alive. You might try an heroic abridgement by saying simply that Greek, like almost all European languages, is an Indo-European language. So far so good.

Of course, there's not a single written account or record of the people who used Proto-Indo-European; when peoples discover writing, they stop using the same language. So, the Greeks, Persians, Hittites, Indians, and every other gang of Indo-Europeans no longer understood one another, even though they all grew out of the same language and were, you might say, linguistic siblings.

Of course, we know neither where nor when this Indo-European "nation" existed, but if its language was so widely distributed, it stands to reason that it was spoken by a cultural dominant majority. As for when, sometime around the second millennium BC (I admit, that's super vague). As for where, between Europe and Asia (even vaguer).

Of course, the passage from Proto-Indo-European to common Greek or proto-Greek (the ancestor of all Greek dialects) is shrouded in mystery. Still, as with Proto-Indo-European, the existence of common Greek implies a cohesive Hellenic civilization with a shared language. An evolved, warlike, and wealthy civilization.

By some accident of history, as scholars so elegantly put it, from the Dark Ages onwards, accounts of the language practically leaped from Proto-Indo-European to various Greek dialects. What happened during the transition we can sum up thus: conquests, transformations to society, power struggles, invasions, and changes of the intellectual ruling class.

You don't still believe in earthquakes, Atlantis, and natural disasters, do you?

They had a completely different mindset than us. In Italian, as in most Romance languages, people make themselves understood by conjugating their verbs. Even a three-year-old knows that "I eat," "I will eat," "I have eaten" and "I ate" are nothing more than different tenses of the verb "to eat." They're a lot alike, to look at them. Right, *at a glance*! In appearance, they're similar. When it comes to Romance languages, to know, we look. Being aware of this is the key to understanding ancient Greek.

The Greeks didn't give a fig that the stems λειπ-, λιπ- and λοιπ- were variations of the verb, λείπω, "to leave." In fact, all of those stems contain such different aspectual meanings that they are almost independent from one another. And—visually speaking—they don't really resemble one another. As in English, the moment "I'm going to leave you" (as long as there's life, there's hope) and the moment "I left you" (keep dreaming, you're on your own) don't resemble one another, and I don't mean just visually.

Maybe a few Greek speakers harbored suspicions, and the wisest among them glimpsed the roots common to the stems of certain verbs, but that was not because they were linguistically aware of them. If anything, it happened despite their being aware.

Homer, for instance, uses verbs in this manner: adopting a stem to express *how* whatever action he wants to describe occurred—or, to be fair, the action that the Muse whispered in his ear. Like the innkeeper in our little tale, the blindman of Chio—or whichever of the six different islands that claim him as their native son—considers, to give just one example, the *tone* of Helen's reaction to being kidnapped by Paris and therefore sparking a war that would last ten years (hint: colossally pissed).

Homer appears oblivious of his choice of stem and more concerned with making himself understood, so that, if we examine the *Iliad* and the *Odyssey*, we notice the great poet appears to be unaware that he is using aspectual variants of the same verb. We see it in the notes to the epic poem and the phalanxes of paradigms in our textbooks—phalanxes we're about as psyched to see as a Greek at Thermopylae.

Homer, and the Greeks in general, didn't make the connection between the various stems of the same verb or, if they did, they didn't pay the connection much mind. Clearly they didn't *feel* it linguistically. Choosing a stem served to get your point across.

To us, the choice can seem mechanical and extremely difficult, and yet they understood one another clearly, maybe more clearly than we do; so often we don't understand one another at all. They certainly communicated with one another with greater precision and candor: they didn't talk to hear themselves talk or act for the hell of it.

If the *Iliad* and the *Odyssey* were the most mainstream epic poems in history and the most effective storytelling tools in Greek society, that means Greeks, no matter their social class, understood them just fine without a PhD in Philology.

Otherwise, were Homer's language meant for a small niche of highly attuned ears, the Greeks would have ditched Homer and raced to find another national poet—just as quickly as we would if sportscasters began giving us a play-by-play of the Super Bowl (with the Rams up in OT!) in Milton's English. We'd change the channel and put a pox on Milton and his England.

Before we examine each stem, I'm going to give an example that will send a shiver up the spine of every student of Greek, past or present, and leave those who don't know a word of Greek speechless. Yet it strikes me as the quickest route to understanding the issue. Certainly, the bravest.

You may have caught wind of the seven verbs called polythematic verbs, which is an elegant way of defining those crazy verbs that break all the rules, verbs that made so much sense to the Greeks that they make no sense at all to us. And those still cuffed to their school desks must have heard of at least three. As is so often the case, in language and in life, we need weirdness to make sense of things. And, well, by looking at these irregular verbs we can see most clearly—*with our own eyes*—the importance of aspect as it pertains to each stem.

Take ὁράω, the most irregular of them all, and for the moment just look at the verb's paradigm as it would appear in any school textbook—present, future, aorist, perfect, passive aorist:

ὁράω, ὄψομαι, εἶδον, οἶδα, ὤφθην

Ironic by design, ὁράω means "to look with one's eyes." So, keep your eyes wide open.

Are you looking closely? You don't need to know how to read Greek. Imagine it's Japanese. See any two words that look alike? Exactly. You don't. Good. Great, actually.

Now take a leap back in time—actual, historical time. Say you found yourself in the agora in Athens and it occurred to you to ask the first person who happened by, "I beg your pardon, but, by Zeus, would you please explain the paradigm of ὁράω?" Odds are the guy would think you were nuts or, worse, a barbarian, and in a matter of minutes you'd either wind up in forced labor or auctioned off at the slave market.

The stems bear such different meanings that they are used independently of one another, and no one cares that οἶδα comes from ὁράω: that's the business of our grammar books. It matters to them exactly as much as it matters to us that the words "patience" and "passion" share the same Latin root. If asked, 99% of the population—to give a generous estimate—would respond, "So? What's it to me?"

Bearing in mind that the purpose of language is to make yourself understood, let's take a look at what the Greeks themselves understood about the various stems of ὁράω:

— ὁράω: "I'm looking" (at an apple, a pretty woman, the sky, a tragedy, whatever I feel like).
— ὄψομαι: "I intend to look, I will look" (as to what is being looked at, see above or look around you).
— εἶδον: "I look."
— οἶδα: "I know"—because I looked carefully and now I know. Period.
— ὤφθην: "I looked"—and someone here knows it.

Another anomalous and therefore illuminating verb is "to say." It only means the same thing as its English equivalent in the aorist form, εἶπον, whereas the present form ranges from ἀγορεύω, "to proclaim publicly," from ἀγορά, "the agora, public square," to λέγω, "I'm choosing, I'm counting." Its perfect stem, εἴρηκα, "I spoke and you all heard me," is totally different and comes from elsewhere.

This semantic range that we've seen at work in the paradigm of ὁράω applies to all Greek verbs. So much so, in fact, that many verbs lack one or more stems, because the meaning of the verb doesn't lend itself to that particular stem. Linguists call the latter defective verbs. For example?

Οἰκέω, "to live, dwell," and βασιλεύω, "to rule over," almost always appear only in the present stem, because the action is always ongoing. You either live somewhere or you're homeless. You're either king or you're not.

Θνήσκω, "to die," only has an aorist stem, because perishing may be the most definitive action of all. The same holds true for βιόω, "to live," when you're grateful just to be alive and can enjoy life whether or not things are perfect.

Ἥκω, my favorite, only has a perfect stem, because it expresses the result of "having left and having finally arrived." I'd translate it with a very unscholarly "Here I am!" But not all professors will appreciate that, so "I've arrived" will do the trick.

Ἔοικα, "to seem, be like," and δέδοικα, "I am afraid," share the same perfect stem, because they are the results of actions that have already taken place. I saw somebody, and they reminded me of someone else. Something occurred, and I got scared. Now is the moment of truth: will you man up or stand down?

From here on out, it's smooth sailing. So here are the various stems explained: enjoy the view. Ah, right, I almost forgot to offer you a glass of (watered-down) wine to raise a toast on your travels. All that follows applies to each mood (indicative, subjunctive, optative, imperative, participle, infinitive, and even the verbal adjective. About this last, no comment; it's rarely taught outside of doctoral programs.)

• **The present stem** is the simplest and applies to the verb as you find it in the dictionary. It indicates an action that is incomplete and still in progress. The speaker has not felt the effect of the action, because they are still living through it, seizing the day, to paraphrase the Romans, an expression that never gets old.

• **The aorist stem** is the marvelous land of ἀόριστος χρόνος, or indefinite time. The word "aorist" itself means without bounds, without a beginning or end. The action is outside of time—specific, unrepeatable; the speaker doesn't question it at all.

The distinction between the present and the aorist is very subtle. So subtle, in fact, that Italians take a bazooka to it in the schools, demanding students translate the aorist with the less conventional remote past (*passato remoto*); sometimes it seems like we're the ones living in the Dark Ages.

Nevertheless, translating a Greek text without being

extremely mindful of the value of the aorist—the "be" looming over all temporal concerns—is risky and, in my opinion, unfortunate.

In English we might employ the beautiful, delicate French word "nuanced" to describe it. Just as the sea contains every kind of blue, the aorist *is* every shade of water, sky, the light playing on the surface, foam, a red freighter in the distance, and, therefore, the Greek language *in toto*.

Basically, the aorist belongs neither to the past nor the present tense, whether active or passive (so we can get rid of that and its suffix, too). It's simply an action to be performed without consideration of the consequences— because there are none, okay? Why must there be?

You could render the idea of unfixed or absolute time with the simple present or periphrasis, like "begin," "succeed," or "burst." So we would have ἐπεθύμησα ("I love"), ὤζησα ("I smell"), ἐχαίρησα ("I am happy"). Which is to say, when one is in love, happy, and smells nice, one simply "is."

There is something spectacular and heartbreaking about the aorist: the certainty of having lost something forever and a blurry regret for that mode of being. The strange nostalgia for things that have not been and never will be experienced.

• **The perfect stem**. The action occurred in the past and its effects continue to be felt in the present. ("We apologize for the inconvenience," as they say over the train's intercom, without ever telling us what exactly the holdup is.)

Here we're in trouble, since the speaker is beset by questions. The perfect mixes things up: the present, because the result refers to the moment you are speaking, and the past, because the action precedes the moment you are speaking.

Translation: the perfect is none other than the tense of the end result, good or bad. That's why translations of Greek verbs in the perfect tense can deviate, sometimes wildly, from the present tense, but to understand this tense, yielding to the present tense (rather than the simple past) best renders the idea of an end that results in a beginning.

We can have a little fun coming up with examples of the perfect as a tense that expresses consequence: ῥιγόω, "I'm cold"; ἐρρίγωκα, "I'm frozen"; πέρθω, "I'm destroying" / πέπορθα, "I have burned it to the ground"; ταράσσω "I'm causing distress" / τέτρηχα, "I've really messed up"; μαίνομαι "I'm getting angry" / μέμηνα, "I'm furious"; κτάομαι, "I'm procuring," and κέκτημαι, "I have." I could go on for a long, long time.

No verb that describes an action that cannot have a consequence takes the perfect stem. First, ἐλπίζω, "I hope—and who knows what'll happen." But the same goes for γελάω, "I'm laughing"; ἀρκέω, "That's enough" or "Stop, I have enough"; ὕω, "It's raining," while either implying the presence of Zeus or explicitly invoking him, since Zeus is the one making the rain, and πτάρνυμαι, "I sneeze."

Neither do most verbs pertaining to music take the perfect stem, because listening to music occurs within an unrepeatable present, whether σαλπίζω, "I'm playing the trumpet,"[4] or ἀλαλάζω, "I'm singing a war song."

What's worse than an action that occurred in the past whose effects continue to be felt in the present? Why the **pluperfect** of course, often called the past perfect in English, when an action that occurred in the past has consequences for another past, consequences that still smolder in the present. The pluperfect is none other than an exacerbated version of the perfect form from which it is derived. It is seldom used, since the Greeks took life in their stride and spoke openly, and there was no point worrying much (as usual, you'll never encounter it until graduate school).

Rarer still is the **future perfect**. Extremely rare, actually. If you come across the future perfect stem in school, chalk it up to bad karma. Projecting future consequences from a present event wasn't a thing for the Greeks, who even shied away from the simple future.

So here goes nothing, the future in Greek explained:

• The **future** doesn't exist. End of story.

The future is built over the present, and there's nothing

---

[4] Since the time of the Indo-Europeans, music has had a momentary and visual value, so much so that one "watched" music rather than listened to it—just as we occasionally attend an unforgettable concert. Every musical event was unrepeatable and unreproducible, because back then it couldn't be uploaded to some device and carried around.

Music required using your eyes and ears. That meaning survives in many wonderful Indian words, like *junun*, Urdu for "the enchanting spell cast by music and a glance," and the album title of Shye Ben Tzur, Jonny Greenwood, and the Rajasthan Express's 2015 masterpiece.

you can do about it. That's right, in ancient Greek the future has no aspect. Or rather, it has an ancient desiderative value that remains clearly recognizable in modern Greek usage. In fact, it is derived from the subjunctive mood to describe a desire, omen, or aspiration, like, for example, "I could be happy," "I would like to be happy." The form was later used to express waiting for an event that had yet to take place and was therefore similar to the future as we imagine it (but with far fewer expectations . . .). For example, χαιρήσω, the future tense of χαίρω, "I'm happy," originally meant "I want to be happy."

The volitional nature of the future emerges with abundant clarity in modern Greek: without a future tense, modern society was forced to make one up. Or reclaim one, actually, with a periphrasis of θα, the verb "to want," followed by the infinitive form. This pretension to the future explains, to borrow Nikos Dimou's phrase, the unhappiness of being Greek (nowadays).

Clearly a brave people, the Greeks didn't dream of asking *how* the future would unfold. There was nothing to question; the future simply had to be experienced. Once experienced, the Greeks appealed to the present, the aorist, and the perfect to talk about it.

Before I stop, one of the most beautiful words in ancient Greek, μέλλω, expresses the simple idea of the future, which could be translated with the simple present: "to be about to." That's it. "I'm about to" in the present. Period. Μέλλω has no other stems; it is both present and future.

To be about to. To live. To be brave. Those afraid, on the other hand, simply "are." That's that.

Now that we've arrived at an understanding of how the Greeks communicated with one another without being tied to time, all we have to figure out is why we don't understand them anymore.

What happened to this language that, when faced with an event, had the advantage and sophistication to consider how, not when? What happened to this somewhat bizarre but beautiful system of stems and aspects? More importantly, how did Greeks become bound to time?

The same answer has circulated for the last two thousand years: barbarians.[5] Aware of the social value of language and that a language changes when the communicative needs of those who speak it change, we can scratch below the surface and add: the transformation of civilization.

Sure, it wasn't all Alexander the Great's fault; the Macedonians' annexation of Greece only provided the engine—and a nifty excuse—for the large-scale diffusion of a linguistic change that was already underway. It's mind-blowing to think that in just a dozen years the

---

[5] The origin of the word barbarian, βάρβαρος, has a clear social and linguistic connotation—very nationalistic and very contemporary, I realize as I write this, thinking about the walls, barbed wire, and borders we insist on retreating behind today. For a Greek, anyone who spoke "bar-bar," that is gibberish, anyone who hadn't mastered the venerable Greek language and blanked when they heard it spoken, was a barbarian. Didn't matter if the barbarian lived on an island near the Aegean. Though not geographically or politically unified until Alexander the Great, the Greeks had always belonged to the same nation, linked by a cultural, religious, and social identity so potent that they could distinguish all other groups of people from themselves with just one word: "barbarian."

Greek people changed the language in which, for several dozen centuries, they had articulated politics, culture, and laws, and invented philosophy, mathematics, astronomy, and drama.

It was replaced by Koine Greek, the lingua franca that, like a phoenix, rose from the ash heap of the Attic dialect and was understood more or less everywhere from the age of Alexander until 1453, the year that the Byzantine Empire fell, the date traditionally attached to the birth of modern Greek.

We now understand the fate of the ancient Greek verb and its stems and why we are totally baffled by the language at first. Those who spoke Koine Greek, which I discuss at greater length later in this book, must have had the same reaction as those of us turning to the first page of our Greek grammar book: too many verbs, too difficult. They didn't understand them well. Hardly understood them at all, in fact!

So, exactly as in Homer's day, the new language leveled out based on society's needs, that is, on what those who spoke it were aiming for. Only this time it was slightly less elevated but traveled much, much farther, spreading from Greece all the way to India.

First, all the verbal anomalies were dropped to make the verb conjugations as simple as possible. Gone the eccentricities that we're now so grateful for because they help us *feel* what we no longer linguistically *hear*.

There goes the aspect, traded in for time. A simplified present lives on without its durative significance.

Polythematic verbs? Irregular stems? In Egypt, where

writing was based on hieroglyphs? Who are we kidding?
Simplify. Regularizing became the one rule.

The aorist endures, yet its longevity is just another form
of surrender. Having callously erased the perfect form[6] from
the board, the aorist shoulders the weight of the perfect's
aspectual meaning and loses its own. Picture this: at the
crossroads of Koine, the aorist and perfect exchange aspectual rucksacks and wander off in different directions. In a
couple of yards, the perfect falls into the ravine of linguistic
history, while the aorist trundles on till it reaches modern
Greek, looking ever more like the simple past. Next, verbs
which *by their nature* didn't have a perfect tense were retro-
fitted with one. In the simplest way possible, of course—by
using the morphological ruins of the aorist.

And the future? Gone too. Well, it never existed in the
first place.

There you have it, the final tally of how people saw the
world and articulated it in words in the age of Koine Greek:
just two stems playing on two opposite and opposing teams.
The present versus the aorist (with a past/perfect meaning)
and the one winner time as we know (and endure) it.

At first, the aspectual value in pre-Koine ancient Greek
is bewildering, like our childhood memories as we grow old.
Like our grandparents' stories, stories about times different
from our own. Yearbooks from years we didn't live through.
Finally, the aspect disappears. Forgotten. Nothing left.

---

[6] The one perfect stem that has survived is the passive participle γραμμένος, "written," and, in an ironic twist of fate, πεθαμένος,
"dead."

After that, we evolved from how things developed to when things happened. Went from seeing in order to understand all that occurs between a beginning and an end, to classifying everything into the past, present, and future. Traveled from how to when. And with aspect gone, we entered the prison of time and clingy, capricious memory.

Linguistically speaking, it's late for us, too late, too much time has passed. We no longer sense the aspect of things nor know how to articulate it in our own grammar. Therefore, we must strive to find another way of giving voice to that particular sense of satisfaction or realization, of longing or desire, which shields every individual from time the destroyer and time the preserver. Like that little flower, the forget-me-not.

GREEK SILENCE:
SOUNDS, ACCENTS, BREATHINGS

> That which others reap is denied
> us, experts of another language.
> If others sow for us, we are
> traveling forever.
>
> Why land if we're always landing
> in opposite harbors?
> Verses remain, fatuous fires fleeing
> the city of the dead.
> —MARIA LUISA SPAZIANI, from *The Eye of the Storm*

"The archaeological ruins are silent." These brilliant, devastating words belong to Antoine Meillet, one of the greatest scholars of the Greek language, in his book *Aperçu d'une histoire de la langue grecque*.

We will never know for certain how a Greek word is pronounced. The sounds of Greek have vanished forever along with those who spoke it. We have their literature, we can read and study them, but we can't pronounce them. They have come down to us silent. Stifled. Voiceless.

Pronunciation is a physical, human fact. The speech organs are positioned in such a way as to make a breath of air vibrate at a particular intensity for a particular length of time. For the pronunciation of ancient Greek there exist written, not human, sources—sources that do not breathe and, therefore, emit no sound. Sources that say without speaking. Approximations of ancient Greek pronunciation have been codified over the centuries. To be able to speak the words, not only read them to yourself. But the sound of ancient Greek has vanished; the words no longer produce noise. The original pronunciation is another fragment of the world of this language that has been lost.

The alphabet with which we now read Greek texts corresponds to the alphabet officially adopted by Athens in 403–402 BC. It is made up of 24 letters (in Greek τὰ γράμματα, from the verb γράφω, "to write"). There are seven vowels (called "pronounceables" in Greek, τὰ φωνήεντα): alpha (α), epsilon (ε), eta (η), iota (ι), omicron (ο), upsilon (υ), and omega (ω). And seventeen consonants (in Greek, τὰ σύμφωνα, or "combined sounds"): beta (β), gamma (γ), delta (δ), zeta (ζ), theta (θ), kappa (κ), lambda (λ), mü (μ), nü (ν), xi (ξ), pi (π), rho (ρ), sigma (σ), tau (τ), phi (φ), chi (χ), psi (ψ). From the names of the first vowel and the first consonant, ἄλφα and βῆτα, we get the word ἀλφάβητος, or "alphabet."

What happens when the words of a language remain but we have no idea how to pronounce them? The written alphabet of ancient Greek remains, not the sound of the letters. Unlike the Indians and Sanskrit, the Greeks didn't have phoneticians who scrupulously analyzed the pronunciation of the language and left behind an accurate description of it. Further, the sounds of Greek range widely over time (from the Archaic Period to the Byzantine Empire) and space (in the various spoken dialects).

The Written Word

The earliest attested example of Greek writing dates back to Mycenaean Greece (XV BC). In 1900, the archaeologist Arthur Evans discovered several clay tablets in the so-called Palace of Minos at Knossos, on the island of Crete, which bear a script referred to as Linear B—to distinguish it from another syllabic script found in Crete called Linear A. Other similar tablets came to light in the Mycenaean palaces in the Peloponnese (Pylos, Mycenae) and on mainland Greece (Thebes and Eleusis).

While the meaning of Linear A remains a mystery, in 1953 linguist John Chadwick and architect and expert cryptographer Michael Ventris deciphered Linear B. It contains the writing of the Greek-speaking Achaean conquerors who succeeded the Minoan civilization. Most of what the tablets bear are inventories of people, objects, gifts and property; it turns out they were administrative, civic, and economic records pertaining to the Mycenaean Civilization. By pure luck, the sun-dried clay tablets were saved after the palaces were burned down during the fall of the Mycenaean civilization.

At the end of the Mycenaean period, Greek writing disappeared for a long time, during the so-called Greek Dark Ages. It reappeared with the introduction of the Phoenician alphabet, the earliest evidence of which dates to the eighth century BC, the very same time that Homer's poems were spread—by word of mouth. The Phoenician alphabet consisted of 22 consonant letters and no vowels. The Greeks retained the Phoenician letters, turned into vowels those signs that expressed sounds that didn't exist in Greek, and added others for diphthongs (ξ, φ, χ, ψ). They

We are, *de facto*, unable to reproduce the original Greek pronunciation. Not only because we don't know what it was like; even if we did, our language doesn't, in fact, possess many phonetic features common to ancient Greek. Greek words are today as silent as the stones of the Acropolis, which tell of an extraordinary world without uttering a word. And if the Greek words did speak, were we also changed the direction of writing from left to right; the Phoenicians wrote from right to left. In the Archaic Period, there is evidence of Boustrophedon writing in Greek, a way of regularly changing direction, one line beginning from the right side, the next from the left (named after the way oxen (βοῦς) turn (στρέφω) when plowing a field). The Greek alphabet of Phoenician origin was simpler and more flexible than their syllabic script. Many more people were able to learn its mechanics, memorize it, reproduce it in writing. That was fundamental for the spread of literacy in the Greek world and the transmission and production of texts, and not just literary texts but texts that served daily needs.

In 403–402 BC, Archinus issued an edict imposing an official Ionic alphabet on Athens and its allied cities. There is evidence that as early as the third century BC, the Athenian alphabet had reached as far as Cyprus, which had long employed a syllabic script similar to the one found in Linear A. The Athenians also communicated their alphabet to non-allied populations they came into contact with, chiefly the Italic people in the Greek colonies. The Etruscans, too, developed a Greek-based alphabet and imparted it to their local populations, from which Latin would derive its own alphabet.

Several centuries later, circa 850 AD, the emperor of Byzantium commissioned two brothers from Thessaloniki, Cyril and Methodius, to evangelize the Slavs. Cyril taught the Slavs a Greek alphabet that originated from Greek cursive script. In the following era, drawing on the Greek uncial script, the Slavic world adopted the alphabet still in use today known as Cyrillic and erroneously attributed to Saint Cyril.

to hear their sound, we wouldn't understand it and would struggle to reproduce it.

Greek was an exceptionally musical language: the same word for the modulation of the accent, prosody, comes from the Greek word for song, πρός ᾠδή. As in English and Italian, the Latin word for accent, *accentus*, comes from *ad cantus*.

Onomatopoeia

As rare as they are weird, examples of onomatopoeia have survived to help give us an idea of how the language was effectively pronounced. We know that in Greek the sheep goes βῆ βῆ (beh beh) and the dog βαύ βαύ (bau bau), from which the verb "to bark" (βαύζειν) is derived, and that to express pain or awe they sighed αἰαῖ (ah!) or οἴ (ow!).

Even weirder is how almost all European onomatopoeic words stem from Greek. In nearly every Romance language, the dog goes *bau bau, bow bow,* or *bow-wow,* and the sheep *bee bee* or *baa baa.* In Russian, on the other hand, the dog goes *gav gav,* in Japanese the sheep goes *meh meh,* and so forth. Though dogs bark and sheep bleat the same way the world over, animal calls are represented by a wide range of onomatopoeia, depending on the presence or absence of particular phonetic sounds in the various languages.

Unlike the majority of European languages, ancient Greek accent (ὁ τόνος) was a melodic or pitch accent, not a stress accent (as can be found in modern-day Chinese, Japanese, and many African languages). Accent depended not so much on stress as on the tone, length, and vibration of the sound emitted; it had a musical intonation. The tonic vowel was characterized by raising, not deepening, one's voice. An accented vowel was more acute than atonic vowels, and the accent had a purely semantic significance. Sometimes, the position of the accent was all that distinguished a word like τόμος (a cut) from τομός (cutting or sharp).

Besides musical, Greek was a strongly rhythmic language. Ancient Greek rhythm is quantitative and based on the alternation of long and short syllables. This is attested to by Greek music, for us an illegible and irreproducible treasure, like the hymns discovered in Delphi meant to be sung and accompanied by music. Every Greek vowel has a short form (ῐ, ε, ᾰ, ο, ῠ) and a long (ῑ, η, ᾱ, ω, ῡ). Combined with ι and υ, the vowels form one syllable (from the Greek word δίφθογγος, "diphthong"). A syllable is inherently short when its vowel is short and not followed by consonants; a syllable is inherently long when its vowel is long or followed by consonants. To determine accent, all that counts are the inherently long and short syllables, i.e., their duration.

On the whole, this rhythmic and musical system of Greek, originating from Indo-European, was robust and lasted dozens of centuries. Because, despite the fact that it remains inaccessible to us today, the pronunciation of Greek was distinct and clear to the Greeks: short or long, tonic or atonic, all the vowels were plainly perceived, such that every syllable was distinct and orderly.

The language's musical accent and rhythm lasted until the second century AD, when the idea of vowel quantity began to fade, and a stress accent emerged, like the one in modern Greek: the vowels aren't inherently long or short but can become so by being accented or not. To this day tonic vowels are pronounced in Greek by raising one's voice, so pitch accent hasn't vanished altogether. What has vanished is the concept of duration.

Already in the third century AD, Greek inscriptions began to confuse vowel length and mistake ε, and η or ο and ω.

The rhythm of the language changed, yet nothing in the written language hints at that change. The speakers themselves probably didn't realize what was going on, as is normal for every irreversible linguistic change. Thus the Greek alphabet was silenced forever, though its forms have remained intact for millennia.

The alphabet has, therefore, escaped the ravages of time. But not only has the original pronunciation been lost forever, the way in which Greek is written has changed over the centuries. A Greek text is difficult, almost impenetrable for us today, though we read it printed clearly on paper and avail ourselves of punctuation, proper spacing, and diacritic marks to get our bearings. But considering that its primary sources—from papyrus to stone epigraphs—utilize a writing practice that is completely different and largely inaccessible in the modern age, the difficulty is relative. (That's why not even a degree in Classics Languages will suffice to read the stones in the Acropolis Museum. For that you'll need a special degree in archeology and epigraphy.)

Up until the third century BC, the Greeks widely employed *scriptio continua*, a style of writing that did not use spaces, different letter cases or diacritics (from διακριτικός, "distinctive") to distinguish one word from another. Translation: at first glance an original Greek text seems to consist of one endless and incomprehensible string of words in all caps. Talk about despair.

When the kind of lowercase writing we read in print today began to spread, the Greeks (rightly) sensed the need to make their texts easier to decipher and began incorporating punctuation. It was the grammarians in the Great Library of Alexandria, during the Hellenistic age that followed the empire of Alexander the Great, who codified the graphic marks that have come down to us: breathings, accents, punctuation. However, their use did not become standardized until several centuries later.

So, if we can now comfortably read a text in ancient Greek, it's all thanks to the Alexandrines. We're indebted to them for the diacritics and punctuation marks that help us comprehend Greek.

They are as follows:

• **Breathing** (πνεῦμα) denotes the absence or presence of aspiration in an initial vowel or diphthong. It can be rough (ʽ) or smooth (ʼ). In the first instance, the word is pronounced with an initial /h/, as for example ὕπνος ("sleep"). The second instance is odd, because Greek goes to the trouble of annotating something that isn't there: the smooth breathing denotes the absence of aspiration, as in εἰρήνη ("peace").

Having waned over the centuries, aspiration vanished with Koine and is altogether absent from modern Greek. It is preserved in Latin but only when transcribing Greek words. That's why the Romans wrote Homerus with an /h/; the name Homer, Ὅμηρος, had a rough breathing.

• **Accent**, which we have seen is by its nature melodic and comes from the word "song," stands on a word's tonic vowel. There are three types: acute (ʹ), grave (ʽ), or circumflex (˜). An acute accent, as its symbol suggests, denotes raising the syllable over which it stands, or rising pitch. A grave accent indicates, as *its* symbol suggests, lowering the syllable, or falling pitch. A circumflex is composed of an acute accent followed by a grave: it indicates a rising pitch followed by a sudden fall. Because it expresses a double rhythm, and lasts twice as long, a circumflex accent can only stand on long vowels or diphthongs, distinguishing it from the first two, which can stand on any vowel.

• **Apostrophe** ('), from ἀποστροφή ("deviation") or ἔκθλιψις ("elimination"), indicates an elision, i.e., dropping the final vowel when the next word begins with a vowel. For example, the Greeks would write οὐδ᾽αὐτός ("that man") for οὐδὲ αὐτός.

• **Iota subscript** is a small stroke or iota (ι) placed below the long vowels ᾳ, ῃ, and ῳ. Its existence suggests that in the classical era there was a diphthong whose second vowel (ι) gradually faded when pronounced and was often, therefore, left untranscribed. In the Byzantine Period, the missing iota was placed below the first vowel of the diphthong rather than next to it. Today the iota subscript is no longer pronounced when reading.

• **Punctuation marks** consisted of the comma (,) and period (.), as in English. The Greeks didn't capitalize letters to begin a new sentence but did at the start of a new passage or chapter.

You'll also find a period above the line (·) indicating a pause longer than a comma but briefer than a period, and often denoted in English with a semicolon; in Greek the semicolon symbol (;) is the equivalent of our question mark.

Contemporary publishers often insert modern punctuation marks into Greek texts, such as quotation marks, colons, and exclamation points, to facilitate reading.

Here, in the modern world, we're of course extremely grateful to the Alexandrines for taking such pains to annotate the breathings, accents, and punctuation marks that didn't exist in ancient Greek and facilitate *our* understanding of the language.

Unfortunately, our infinite gratitude is equal to our infinite stupidity—in order to benefit from the aid of these diacritics, we first have to understand them. Often, almost always, we don't understand them at all, such that these marks, meant to assist our understanding of a text, turn into yet another obstacle, a first hurdle, confusion from the get-go—in other words, they put us at a clear disadvantage. Now, we're not so stupid that we can't figure out commas, spaces, and apostrophes: up to that point we're good. But breathings and accents are another matter altogether, an infuriating matter for those who know what I'm talking about as well as for those who don't. In school, the first thing you learn in a few weeks of Greek lessons is the alphabet. How proud and excited we are as we learn to read and write for a second time in this life! How excited to copy out those first, unfamiliar Greek letters by hand, uppercase and lower! What satisfaction we take in composing our first crooked syllables or transliterating our own names in an alphabet different from our own and then in showing our friends and relatives with staggering conceit. How gratified we are to say our first word out loud, our voices shaky—why do we never remember the first word we spoke in another language?

The pride, excitement, satisfaction, and gratification last as long as it takes to turn the page in our grammar book and find the chapter with which every Greek grammar book worthy of the name begins: Phonetics. That's when we make the painful discovery that pops our balloon: you can't read and write Greek by knowing the alphabet alone. You need to know and study the laws that govern its accents and breathings.

Laws—that's exactly what they're called; those things that impose rules in exchange for rights. Except those rights, the aids to our understanding, almost invariably turn out to be useless, because we no longer understand them.

I've never met a single beginning student of Greek who wasn't unconfident, clumsy, desperate, or stumped by the laws of accents, the same accents that, according to the Alexandrines, were supposed to help us understand the text. I, for one, was stumped. And I'm still stumped.

I remember clearly my first exam at the end of my first year in high school. I remember the blank page on which I had perfectly transcribed, conjugated, and inflected the verbs and nouns my teacher asked me to. I even remember—how could I ever forget—which they were: the verb γράφω ("to write") and the noun ἡ οἰκία ("home"). But what I most remember is the blind, mad, relentless desperation that came over me when I remembered that I had to accent and aspirate those words—what the hell did "aspirate" even mean? What a nightmare! The bell was ringing, I'd aced my exam, it was beyond reproach, the grammar book had nothing on me. But . . . the breathings and accents were missing. Looking up during a test was the same as asking to be publicly shamed in a class of fourteen-year-olds who lived to see other people humiliated. I can't go on. I'm desperate. Not in a million years. I'm going to cry. That's all I could think of. So I kept my eyes glued to my sheet of paper and weighed my options.

Should I leave the words mutilated, with no breathings or accents? No way. That would have been like going to a designer store to try on shoes and having holes in your socks. Randomly stick them in? How randomly? I searched my knapsack of knowledge on the subject. Nice and light. *A smooth breathing looks like the belly of a 'D.'* I'll never forget those ridiculous tricks we were taught in high school! *The belly of a 'D.' After* si, nisi, num *and* ne, ali- *takes a holiday.* Even the teacher blushed to utter those linguistic chestnuts, and you swore you'd never in your life repeat them, only to find yourself a couple years later proudly proclaiming them to your students. Because those chestnuts work. Even after having confirmed that the sweet breathing was the one with a belly, and the rough was, by default, anorexic, the question remained: where the heck did you put them?

To say nothing of accents—those were even worse. Because in two million years the trick to distinguishing acute from grave had yet to be invented. The plural genitive was discarded, circumflex went there—of that much I was sure. Maybe the dative too. But the dual? How did you explain the dual?

For a moment I was deeply irked at the Alexandrines for

inventing accents and breathings. The Greeks hadn't needed them. Thanks, thanks a lot—spare yourself the trouble next time, we're good here. I had to give in. My time was up. With a serious and determined, persnickety and fanatical look on my face, I affixed breathings and accents to each word. Confident, cavalier, my hand sped across the test, slapping a comma here and a comma there. Of course, I got them all wrong.

When it comes to breathings and accents, I clearly represent a particularly grave case of doltishness—clinical, you might say. I never learned them the way I was supposed to, not even in college. I studied hard to put things right, learned the rules, practiced like mad. But all my efforts were in vain, because I never let up. I won the battle to understand them but lost the war to understand their point. If we'll never know the original pronunciation of Greek, why bother learning a bogus version?[7] Moreover, why bother putting it in writing? What if English were to vanish from the face of the earth and all that was left was the written word? How could anyone imagine, or worse, codify English pronunciation based exclusively on the works of Shakespeare and Twain—or, why'll we're at it, on Facebook posts and the Twittersphere?

As for rough and smooth vowel breathings, there's little

---

[7] Italian schools follow the system of pronunciation advocated by Erasmus of Rotterdam in *Dialogus de recta Latini Graecique sermonis pronuntiatione* (Basel, 1528). This pronunciation is sometimes called etacism, after the letter η, or "eta." The humanist Giovanni Reuchlin advocated another type of pronunciation, called Reuchilinian or itacism, because the letter η is pronounced "ita." This pronunciation is modeled on Byzantine and modern Greek and has been adopted in Greece and other countries.

to do: study a little, memorize a little, intuit a ton. Generally speaking, even were we to know the breathing of every Greek word beginning with a vowel, we would no longer be able to pronounce the aspiration that goes with it. "We don't pronounce it in Italian"—that's how the grammar books in my country wash their hands of this business. And many teachers still define breathings and accents as ornamental: dashes and scores that make the words look more elegant but are otherwise superfluous—like some beautiful women, all dolled up and almost unreal.

As for accents, there actually are many highly complicated laws, given that Greek is a musical language, possibly reserved for people with a strong sense of rhythm, which I, apparently, don't possess (I can't even dance to Latin music). The most common—and most reliable lifeline—is the law of three syllables, also known as the Law of Limitation, because it proceeds by exclusion. If the final syllable of a word is short, the accent may fall as early as the antepenultimate syllable (so we have three possibilities). If the last syllable is long, the accent may fall as early as the penultimate (two possibilities).

Our incomprehension and discomfort when faced with Greek breathings and accents stems from our having lost the pronunciation of the language. Its characteristic melody and musical rather than stress-based rhythm are completely alien to us. Our ears will never pick up ancient Greek from a native speaker—which is one of the ways we learn as children to pronounce words correctly in our own language, or how to say "good morning" correctly in a foreign language before ever knowing how to write.

That's why those written marks introduced by the Alexandrines to facilitate our reading of Greek are, for us, so hard: they knew how to read Greek and we don't. At the same time, the Alexandrines have enabled us to stammer our way through Greek and rescued it for us from eternal silence. Endeavor as we may to study and understand it, the truth is that we'll never arrive at hearing how a long or brief vowel or an acute, grave or circumflex accent should sound. We can only sort of hear it—and imagine. That is to say, we must. Because, if we don't make the effort that Greek phonetics requires, one of the greatest gifts of Greek will remain forever out of reach: poetry.

Greek poetry—epic, lyric, tragic, comic—contains all there is to know about the intensity of human experience.

In English we might know how to read heroic couplets, sonnets, ballads, pentameter lines, hexameter lines, and blank verse (since the accents are our own), but how did they compose poetry in Greek? More importantly, how did they read it?

The rhythm of the language was based on alternating long and short syllables, and accents took a backseat. In ancient Greece, composing a verse meant parceling out long and short syllables in a regular manner. The poets didn't, therefore, focus on the tone of words while versifying but on the rhythm and duration—long or short—of their syllables. From the Archaic period until the post-Christian era, they never tried to match the *times* of their verses with accents. Poeticizing was completely indifferent to the placement of accents.

The Greeks perceived both accent and syllable length for any chosen meter. Unable to perceive both, we're the ones who resort to counting the stresses when we scan poetry. What mattered then was the melodic sound of the language, musicality as a sincere mode of expression, the carefully chosen order of long and short syllables.

Which is why it is impossible to claim that Greek poetry, whether it be by Homer, Pindar, Sappho, Sophocles or Aristophanes, was only recited; its musicality excludes an oral reading comparable to that of English poetry. At the same time, Greek poetry wasn't just sung either, even if poets were occasionally accompanied by a string instrument, like the lyre or cithara.

The melody of Greek poetry was connected to the musical nature of their language, the continuous modulations and dips of the speaker's voice, the length with which each syllable of a verse was pronounced. That musicality can be detected, even if less distinctly, in prose too.

Precise metrical patterns, or modes of making verse based on diverse rhythms, existed for specific poetic genres. For example, hexameter for the epic; iambic, trochaic, and Aeolic meters for the lyric; iambic trimeter for tragedies and comedies, with the chorus sung in Aeolic verse. None of these patterns, which are extremely difficult for us to understand and render, corresponded to one characteristic of the Greek language alone: they also corresponded to each poet's expressive choice. The possibility of substituting a long vowel for two short vowels, in fact, amplified the range of words that the poets chose to versify and made them more natural. Greek poetry didn't shoehorn the language into meter; it was a way of giving voice to a certain idea of the world—a musical world.

When our grasp of the quality of syllables got lost, around the third century AD, there was just one way of preserving that world: by annotating it. That it was silent didn't matter. By the Byzantine Era, our grasp of original metrical forms had slipped completely, yet grammarians continued to copy out their metrical patterns, page after page. Thanks to their tireless, silent tenacity, the remnants of Greek meter survived the fall of Constantinople and have been passed down to us.

So, how did the sounds of Greek poetry reach us concretely? If you could photograph a silent language, it would look something like this:

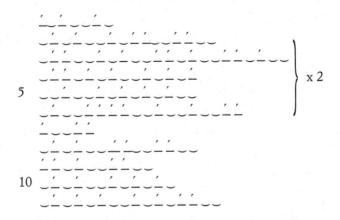

This is the written representation of the metrical pattern used by the poet Pindar in Pythian X, dedicated to Hippocles. True, the symbol (‾) marks a long vowel and the symbol (˘) a short one. True, underneath these symbols, there are words that carry meaning and were chosen to celebrate Hippocles' feats and mythic origins. Yet it's just as true that even if we endeavor to understand the meter, even if we place accents over the long vowels in our own way (i.e., tonally), we'll never approach an understanding of how this poetry was pronounced.

We'll never understand exactly why the poet chose to alternate short and long, or what he meant to express by those choices. For us, this poetry is silent. We have lost a fundamental part of its meaning.

Like fish in a bowl, we move our lips without emitting a sound. Or at least not a Greek sound.

> We can never hope to get the whole fling of a sentence in Greek as we do in English. We cannot hear it, now dissonant, now harmonious, tossing sound from line to line across a page. We cannot pick up infallibly one by one all those minute signals by which a phrase is made to hint, to turn, to live. Nevertheless, it is the language that has us most in bondage; the desire for that which perpetually lures us back.

So writes Virginia Woolf in "On not Knowing Greek."

And that's how things stand. We can never hope to make the intensity of a single word in ancient Greek our own. Yet we continue to study this language, which has lured us for millennia, with the power of distance that, for millennia, we have mistaken or swapped for proximity. In the Greek texts we no longer read the Greek world; we read ourselves.

The same holds true for the musicality of Greek, which we now read with our sounds and our rhythms. But we'd give anything to hear, even just once, how a Greek word was really pronounced. A record with no record player. Having lost the needle, not knowing how to balance the tonearm, we must imagine the sound to feel the music.

THREE GENDERS, THREE NUMBERS

> And we are the shore
> but always this side of that island
> where one says "I" to say
> —to be—"we."
> —PIERLUIGI CAPPELLO, from *Elementary Blue*

In Italian, we only have two genders with which to put a human face, shade, and nature on the world: masculine and feminine. In English, apart from naturally gendered nouns and pronouns, there is none. Ancient Greek had three: masculine, feminine, and neuter.

In Italian, we only have two numbers with which to measure our lives: the singular and plural. Ancient Greek had a third: the dual.

I have searched far and wide for a page in ancient Greek that could help readers connect with these lost grammatical genders and numbers. I turned over anthologies, scoured texts. I worked breathlessly, but nothing struck me as re-velatory enough for readers to understand or hear it. On the one hand, it's practically impossible to find a single line of ancient Greek where the neuter does not appear. Its overexposure blinds those seeking to understand it. On the other, dual number is so rarely used that it's practically impossible to find more than one line in which it appears with any consistency. Its *under*exposure blinds those seeking to understand it.

In the end, I decided on one of the most famous passages in Plato, a passage commonly cited to talk about the twin souls or two halves of the same sorb-apple. (I chose this passage also because, well, how many people have *actually* read the passage, and not just on a slip of paper inside a chocolate wrapper?) In short, I chose a passage that talks about love. Or solitude. Because, sooner or later in life, we all experience love, and we all experience the end of love—abandonment.

I'm aware that, even though gender-neutral words and the dual appear here, this isn't the most orthodox example for illustrating this particular quirk of the Greek language. I'm aware that the text means to talk about something else: love, actually. But by now *you* should have figured out that the book you're holding isn't a Greek grammar book but an unconventional tale about Greek grammar.

The word "to translate" is derived from the Latin word *traducto*, meaning to convey or carry across. That's what I mean to do with this passage from the *Symposium*: carry readers, regardless of whether they've studied Greek, over to a land of genders and grammatical numbers that they may no longer recognize. Carry them to the other shore and leave them to imagine and listen so that they may understand it:

Πρῶτον μὲν γὰρ τρία ἦν τὰ γένη τὰ τῶν ἀνθρώπων,

οὐχ ὥσπερ νῦν δύο, ἄρρεν καὶ θῆλυ, ἀλλὰ καὶ τρίτον προσῆν κοινὸν ὂν ἀμφοτέρων τούτων, οὗ νῦν ὄνομα λοιπόν, αὐτὸ δὲ ἠφάνισται.

In the first place, there were three kinds of human beings, not merely the two sexes, male and female, as at present: there was a third kind as well, which had equal shares of the other two, and whose name survives though the thing itself has vanished.

Ἔπειτα ὅλον ἦν ἑκάστου τοῦ ἀνθρώπου τὸ εἶδος στρογγύλον, νῶτον καὶ πλευρὰς κύκλῳ ἔχον, χεῖρας δὲ τέτταρας εἶχε, καὶ σκέλη τὰ ἴσα ταῖς χερσίν, καὶ πρόσωπα δύ᾽ ἐπ᾽ αὐχένι κυκλοτερεῖ, ὅμοια πάντῃ.

Secondly, the form of each person was round all over, with back and sides encompassing it every way; each had four arms, and legs to match these, and two faces perfectly alike on a cylindrical neck.

Ἦν δὲ διὰ ταῦτα τρία τὰ γένη καὶ τοιαῦτα, ὅτι τὸ μὲν ἄρρεν ἦν τοῦ ἡλίου τὴν ἀρχὴν ἔκγονον, τὸ δὲ θῆλυ τῆς γῆς, τὸ δὲ ἀμφοτέρων μετέχον τῆς σελήνης, ὅτι καὶ ἡ σελήνη ἀμφοτέρων μετέχει.

The number and features of these three sexes were owing to the fact that the male was originally the off-spring of the sun, and the female of the earth; while that which partook of both sexes was born of the moon, for the moon also partakes of both.

Ἦν οὖν τὴν ἰσχὺν δεινὰ καὶ τὴν ῥώμην, καὶ τὰ φρονήματα μεγάλα εἶχον, ἐπεχείρησαν δὲ τοῖς θεοῖς, καὶ ὃ λέγει Ὅμηρος περὶ Ἐφιάλτου τε καὶ Ὤτου, περὶ ἐκείνων λέγεται, τὸ εἰς τὸν οὐρανὸν ἀνάβασιν ἐπιχειρεῖν ποιεῖν, ὡς ἐπιθησομένων τοῖς θεοῖς. ὁ οὖν Ζεὺς καὶ οἱ ἄλλοι θεοὶ ἐβουλεύοντο ὅτι χρὴ αὐτοὺς ποιῆσαι, καὶ ἠπόρουν.

Now, they were of surprising strength and vigour, and so lofty in their notions that they even conspired against the gods; and the same story is told of them as Homer relates of Ephialtes and Otus, that scheming to assault the gods in fight they essayed to mount high heaven.

Thereat Zeus and the other gods debated what they should do, and were perplexed.

Μόγις δὴ ὁ Ζεὺς ἐννοήσας λέγει ὅτι 'δοκῶ μοι', ἔφη, 'ἔχειν μηχανήν, ὡς ἂν εἶέν τε ἄνθρωποι καὶ παύσαιντο τῆς ἀκολασίας ἀσθενέστεροι γενόμενοι. Νῦν μὲν γὰρ αὐτούς, ἔφη, διατεμῶ δίχα ἕκαστον, καὶ ἅμα μὲν ἀσθενέστεροι ἔσονται, ἅμα δὲ χρησιμώτεροι ἡμῖν διὰ τὸ πλείους τὸν ἀριθμὸν γεγονέναι· καὶ βαδιοῦνται ὀρθοὶ ἐπὶ δυοῖν σκελοῖν'.

Then Zeus, putting all his wits together, spake at length and said: "Methinks I can contrive that men, without ceasing to exist, shall give over their iniquity through a lessening of their strength. I propose now to slice every one of them in two, so that while making them weaker we shall find them more useful by reason of their multiplication; and they shall walk erect upon two legs."

Ταῦτα εἰπὼν ἔτεμνε τοὺς ἀνθρώπους δίχα, ὥσπερ οἱ

τὰ ὅα τέμνοντες καὶ μέλλοντες ταριχεύειν, ἢ ὥσπερ οἱ τὰ ᾠὰ ταῖς θριξίν.

So saying, he sliced each human being in two, just as they slice sorb-apples to make a dry preserve, or eggs with hairs;

Ὁ ἔρως ἔμφυτος ἀλλήλων τοῖς ἀνθρώποις καὶ τῆς ἀρχαίας φύσεως συναγωγεὺς καὶ ἐπιχειρῶν ποιῆσαι ἓν ἐκ δυοῖν καὶ ἰάσασθαι τὴν φύσιν τὴν ἀνθρωπίνην.

Thus anciently is mutual love ingrained in mankind, reassembling our early estate and endeavouring to combine two in one and heal the human sore.[8]

SOULFUL OR SOULLESS: NEUTER

Man, woman. Sky, earth, sea. Mouth, thought. Tree, fruit.

Ancient Greek had an intense way of putting a face on the world. It had a way of evaluating nature by digging miles and miles under the surface. Besides feminine and masculine nouns, which Romance languages retain, the Greeks had an extra gender: neuter.

The division was not based on the "colors" of words: not on the pink and blue of children, nor on the absence of color, like black or white. The division wasn't even based on sex—otherwise, which gender would "thoughts" be? Ancient Greek divided gender into animate (masculine

8 Plato, *Symposium*, trans. W. R. M. Lamb, Loeb Classical Library 166 (Cambridge, MA: Harvard University Press, 1925), 134–136.

or feminine) and inanimate. The things of this world were grammatically classified "With Soul" or "Without Soul." Neuter was used for abstract concepts: τὸ ὄνομα (name), τὸ μέτρον (measure), τὸ δῶρον (gift), τὸ θέατρον (theater). For some objects: τὸ ὅπλον (weapon), τὸ δόρυ (spear). And for some entities: τὸ ὄρος (mountain), τὸ ὕδωρ (water), τὸ κῦμα (wave). The human body, τὸ σῶμα, was neuter, as were body parts: τὸ ἦτορ (heart), τὸ πρόσωπον (face), τὸ δάκρυον (tears). Spring (ἔαρ) was neuter, and dreams were neuter (τὰ ὀνείρατα).

The division of two types, animate (masculine or feminine) and inanimate (neuter), derives from Proto-Indo-European and is plainly preserved in Greek. But most animate nouns were not even sorted into masculine and feminine in Proto-Indo-European inflection: they were a single gender, sharing the same, animated world view. It was Greek that made distinctions between them when it added masculine and feminine articles.

Neuter stood in stark contrast to the other two genders, and that contrast survived the entirety of ancient Greek history, and Koine, with only the occasional confusion and ambivalence, and has arrived in present-day Greek intact and charged with meaning.

For once, a quirk of ancient Greek that hasn't been erased from the whiteboard of history! The distinction between animate and inanimate, the Indo-European mindset itself, has, for millennia, retained its grammatical and functional role. Having outlived wars, invasions, and ancient history, neuter has been passed down to us, to recent history. Or rather, it was passed down to (modern) Greeks, for, unlike some Germanic languages, neuter disappeared from all the Romance languages that are derived from Latin. With the successive arrivals of new civilizations, every word in the Romance languages had to be categorized into masculine or feminine. Buried under the rubble of the Roman Empire, each word quit asking itself whether it had soul or not. Linguistically speaking, masculine and feminine became the only way to distinguish things.

Life, ὁ βίος, is masculine. Death, ὁ θάνατος, is masculine. "Being alive," τὸ ζῷον, is neuter.

In short, the system of three Greek genders was based on an ancient distinction between animate words and inanimate words—soulless or soulful. Why one word was masculine and another feminine was far less clear; its original significance had become remote, fuzzy, diminished. The Greek word for gender itself, τὸ γένος, is neuter.

The distinction between neuter and masculine/feminine is more meaningful than you might imagine. Often it is hard to track down and grasp the reason why a Greek word is a certain gender; sometimes it is impossible. Because they generate life, trees are feminine, like Mother Earth. But their fruits, which are seen linguistically as objects, are neuter. So "pear tree" (ἡ ἄπιον) is feminine, while "pear" (τό ἄπιον) is neuter. "Fig" (τό σῦκον) is neuter, but the tree that bears figs, ἡ συκέα, is feminine. The word that stands for both "olive" and "olive tree" (ἡ ἔλαιον) is feminine, while "olive oil" (τό ἔλαιον) is neuter.

Isidore of Seville

No discussion of the fall of the Roman Empire and linguistic ruins, is complete without a mention of Isidore of Seville, the most brilliant, erudite, and weird language scholar of the Dark Ages.

It is actually on account of his unparalleled originality that Saint Isidore of Seville (560–636 AD), Doctor of the Church, warrants mention here—mention that will never be sufficient, given all of the books and ideas that Isidore rescued from his own tumultuous times and passed down to us.

One way of honoring his boundless courage, and equally boundless imagination, is to read the *Etymologiae,* or *Origines*, his compendium of universal knowledge, from medicine to language, geography to zoology, the arts to the law. In fact, Isidore of Seville's *Etymologiae* is the first ency-clopedia and one of the greatest records of Greco-Roman culture before its ultimate collapse. As languages, nations, laws, religions, and states were changing, as people's understanding of Latin was becoming increasingly fuzzy, and all memory of Greek was being forgotten in Western Europe, his work was read, copied, and taught throughout the Middle Ages.

In the opening chapter of Book IX, which addresses the languages of various nations, Isidore of Seville writes with extraordinary foresight: "It is asked what language human beings will speak in the future; the an-swer is nowhere to be found. The Apostle says, 'Or tongues shall cease.' Therefore, we have treated languages first, and then nations, because nations arose from languages, and not languages from nations."[9]

In Canto X of the *Paradiso*, with great conviction, Dante calls the

9 *The Etymologies of Isidore of Seville*, ed. and trans. Stephen Barney et al. (Cambridge, UK: Cambridge University Press, 2006).

Diminutives of masculine and feminine words are neuter and can be used affectionately or disparagingly. Ὁ μόσχος is a "calf," τό μοσχίον a "baby calf." Ὁ μεῖραξ is a "boy," τό μειράκιον a "little boy."

breath of Isidore "ardent," as the Spaniard does not shy from the titanic effort of describing all of reality by examining the origin of words.

Isidore's effort wasn't in vain, if you consider that, while libraries in the Dark Ages were going up in smoke, and ancient texts with them, people who had once shared a language for centuries and were now being split apart, people who found themselves at a crossroads between the past and the present, were able to learn about the ancient world thanks to his *Etymologiae*.

There's no denying that many of his etymologies are bizarre, fanciful, pure invention (and therefore delicious to read today). Delicious to read, yes, but they are not for us to judge. Nowadays we have access to all sorts of information and scientific knowledge, but Isidore of Seville was rescuing what he could while a political and, more importantly, cultural empire was collapsing under his feet. We should praise his efforts and his imagination.

In Chapter 7 of Book I, "Grammar," Isidore affirms that the two genders are masculine and feminine.

With typical scruple, he also mentions "special" genders produced by human rationality: neuter nouns (from *ne-uter*, "neither the one nor the other"); common nouns, which could be either gender, like *canis*, which means both "male dog" and "female dog"; and a very weird epicene gender used to indicate both sexes. About this last, Isidore provides an almost exhaustive explanation. He uses "fish" as an example and writes that it is only masculine because "the sex of this animal is uncertain, since it cannot be distinguished by nature or by sight, but only by expert hands."

One last note. In 2002, Pope John Paul II declared Isidore of Seville patron saint of the Internet and IT professionals. His *Etymologiae*, which gathers together all human knowledge, can be seen as a precursor of the web, and its orderly index of subjects as the first database in history.

Ἡ πρᾶξις, "praxis or the practice of doing," is feminine, while the outcome of that practice, τό πρᾶγμα, "a thing done," is neuter. "Earth" (γῆ) and "sea" (θάλασσα) are feminine, since both embody life, generation, fertility, and, therefore, soul.

Sometimes, singular nouns that are masculine or feminine, and therefore animate, become neuter in the plural form, because collectively they express abstract ideas. "Road" (ἡ κέλευθος) is feminine, while "sea route" or "voyage" (τά κέλευθα) is neuter. "A torch" (ὁ λύχνος) is masculine; "light" (τά λύχνα) is neuter.

Why some parts of the body are masculine, some feminine, and others neuter remains unclear. "Eye" (ὁ ὀφθαλμός), "tooth" (ὁ ὀδούς) and "foot" (ὁ πούς) are masculine. "Nose" (ἡ ῥίς) and "hand" (ἡ χείρ) are feminine. "Mouth" (τό στόμα), "ear" (τό οὖς), and "knee" (τό γόνυ) are neuter.

In ancient Greek, many archaic words that refer to the land, agriculture, and husbandry resort to one animate gender without making distinctions between the sexes.

Ὁ/Ἡ βοῦς means both "ox" and "cow"; ὁ/ἡ ἵππος "stallion" *and* "mare." The sex could then be specified with the adjective and article, or specific words like ὁ ταῦρος, "bull."

In some cases, for no logical reason, there are both a masculine and feminine form of the same word: ὁ γόνος and ἡ γονή both mean "offspring."

In Greek, gender, along with number, establishes the relationships between words within a given phrase. For a language built around a case system, it is of considerable grammatical importance and plays a fundamental role where syntax is concerned, binding the appropriate words together.

As any student will tell you, gender and number are a great help when getting your bearings in a Greek text, a compass on your hunt for meaning.

How is the difference between masculine, feminine,

and neuter studied in school? How are grammatical genders learned?

When it comes to gender, nothing in our collective memory can help us (unless you're crazy enough to memorize every word in the dictionary!). Nor is there a perfect method for teaching it, not even to the most linguistically astute and attentive.

Why a word is either masculine or feminine (or neuter) is, no matter the language, hard to glean or explain. The real reason is that every language, living or dead, chooses gender—when it chooses gender at all—in an almost utterly arbitrary fashion. Native speakers pick it up, hear it *in their hearts* as they piece together their words, and are often oblivious as to what they're doing. But when it comes to ancient Greek, which today is nobody's native tongue, the gender of words doesn't dwell inside us. There are no surviving speakers, only texts—it is thus a mute inheritance.

As a consequence, there is neither an automatic nor a systematic way to figure out the gender of ancient Greek words. Each is masculine, feminine, or neuter because it sounded that way to the ears and minds of those who spoke that language.

Gender, therefore, is exclusively determined by the language—in every language—and there's nothing you can do about it. It is a completely unique way of articulating the world. For example, the sea is masculine in Italian (*il mare*) and feminine in French (*la mer*). No speaker stops to ask why or considers it strange: in both cases, it comes naturally.

Inversely, every speaker flies into a panic and struggles to study gender in a foreign language. Learning gender in ancient Greek isn't so different from learning the genders in other languages. Almost nothing depends on sensibility; in fact, comparing it to your mother tongue can be the quickest way to make a colossal fool of yourself. Almost everything depends on unpredictability.

It takes patience, persistence, latitude, and attitude. It takes time, all the time necessary. The more often you come across a word in your Greek studies, be it masculine or feminine or neuter, the better your chances of remembering its gender.

Most of all, it takes faith, in yourself and in the language, which *is what it is* and, because of that, special.

One example of how arbitrary genders can be? My name, Andrea.

Etymologically, Andrea is derived from the Greek word for "male" (ὁ ἀνήρ). And that's exactly what it means—no excuses, exceptions, or right to appeal.

But as luck would have it, I'm a woman.

But as luck would have it, I'm the daughter of a man for whom fear and sadness are foreign words, someone who greets every sunrise grateful to be alive, and who had the illogical but glorious idea of calling me Andrea. "Just Andrea," he boomed—or so they say—when the baffled clerk at the registry office suggested adding a more "traditional" middle name.

And as a woman raised in Italy, I can assure you that growing up with a boy's name was no laughing matter. Or rather, it was a matter of nonstop laughter at my expense. In Italy, my name has always been seen as a boy's name. There's not a lot you can do about that. Whatever my mother told me when I'd come home humiliated was little consolation. "Andrea ends with an 'a,'" she'd say. "That kind of makes it feminine." But I wanted a name like other girls' names, one that was all feminine, not "kind of." When I was six or seven, I even took to lying, telling people my name was Silvia, which broke my father's heart.

Telling me a hundred thousand times that in half of Europe, not to mention North and South America, Andrea was a girl's name, was especially pointless. Nothing mattered—not even the fact that, clearly, I am a woman. Andrea is a boy's name in Italy, and that's how all Italians hear it. Period. Maybe not across the border, but here, yes. This linguistic *sentiment* explains why every day, without fail, someone says to me, "You're not from around here, are you?" (My blond hair, blue eyes, and pale skin never helped either; even today, there's always somebody at a café who will address me in English or German.)

Then there's the IRS, who assigned me the wrong *codice fiscale*—a national and fiscal ID number—so that when I turned eighteen, I received my military conscription card. Like every Italian boy at the time.

Whenever I introduce myself, depending on the situation, I am met with awkward silence, a variety of grunts ("Huh?" or "Ah"), questions for clarification (*"Andrea* Andrea?"), or, in the worst-case scenario, a corny joke. One time, somebody was so convinced that Andrea was a pen name that they demanded to know my real name (why I'd need to go by a pen name then was anybody's guess.)

Every time I use a credit card bearing my name, the cashier looks at me as if I were a thief or, if I'm lucky, asks if my husband knows that I'm shopping on his dime. The ticket inspector on the train, embarrassed, will clear his throat and force me to reassure him that, yes, "It's me." And the flight attendant will invariably ask to see my ID three times—for security's sake.

Not one call-center operator ever believes that I'm Andrea. Ditto postal workers, bank tellers, ticket-takers at stadiums or concert venues. But it's me, that's right, even if in Italy my name is a man's name.

On account of my name, I average about three misunderstandings a day, so you can imagine my relief whenever I set foot abroad (right now I'm writing in Sarajevo, where, given my name and complexion, as far as anybody's concerned, I'm Slavic.)

And yet, once I grew up to be a woman I became proud of the name Andrea, however odd it is for a Greek scholar to have an etymologically aberrant name.

Andrea is my name, my way of being, my flag. I thank my dad for his strength and his independent spirit—aside from cheerfulness, it's been his most beautiful gift to me. That it is a boy's name doesn't matter. Remember I said that the genders of things are natural and dwell inside us? Well, I'm so used to wearing my name that sometimes it seems impossible to me that a man could be called Andrea!

I, WE TWO, WE: DUAL

Eyes, ears, hands, feet.
    Brothers, friends, allies.
    Lovers.

THE INGENIOUS LANGUAGE · 85

Grammatically speaking, ancient Greek counted to three: one, two, and two or more.

In addition to "I" and "we," the numbers with which we count things, i.e., the numbers with which we measure all life, ancient Greek had a third number: dual, "we two." Two eyes (τὼ ὄμματε), two hands (τὼ χεῖρε), two brothers (τὼ ἀδελφὼ), two horses (τὼ ἵππω). Most of all, two people (τὼ ἀνθρώπω).

The dual didn't merely express a mathematical equation: not one plus one equals two. For life's ordinary arithmetic there already existed the plural, just as there does today. The dual expressed a twinned entity: one plus one equals one formed by two intimately linked things or people. The dual is the number of connection, agreement, mutual understanding. It's the number of natural-born couples or couples that chose to be together.

The dual is the number both of alliance and exclusion. Two isn't just a couple. Two is also the opposite of one and thus the opposite of solitude. It's as if there were a large enclosure: Those inside the dual recognize it. Those outside are barred for good. You're either in or out.

Like aspect, the dual arrives in ancient Greek via the linguistic stores of Indo-European. Therefore, it is an ancient, pure number. A way of making numerical sense of the world. Latin, from which Romance languages derive, immediately drops it; even its earliest texts don't bear the slightest trace of the dual. On the other hand, the dual can be found in Sanskrit as well as in current Lithuanian and Slavic languages. Semitic languages also employ the dual, as does modern Arabic.

The dual wasn't an outlier in ancient Greek. It wasn't a mathematical whim in the language and those who spoke it. The number was deliberately adopted, both in the nominative inflection and for all persons of the verbal inflection, every time one spoke of two people or two things that were united. They may have been a natural pair, like eyes or hands, or else joined for a moment, like lovers. Yet as far back as Homer's time, the dual tends to become murky and confusing, to disappear and reappear depending on the—sometimes very liberal—use an author makes of it. For the Greeks, the dual resided in a realm where it made sense, where the speaker *felt* it. And yet Proto-Indo-European archaisms, the relics of a dead language, immediately vanished from the idiom of the day.

The dual was a way of counting the world, taking stock of the nature of things and the relationships between them. It was a very concrete number, very *human*. Like life, it was intuitive, and its logic varied from case to case. The dual was the least boring of numbers, hard to classify, impossible to normalize.

When Greek civilization grew more complex, Greek numbers turned from concrete to abstract. Firmly logical numbers. Unerringly quantifiable numbers, which didn't bind together things that were joined one moment but might be separated the next. *Linguistically* mathematical numbers. The language changes when those who speak it change.

The dual vanished from most colonies the moment they were founded, since the rate of progress there was faster, and, as is often the case, linguistically harried. On the island of Lesbos, Sappho ignores the dual—as do all others who spoke Ionian dialect. Conversely, the dual held firm in rural mainland Greece, where its connection to the land made it harder, slower to forget the grammatical number.

The dual was most prevalent in the Attic dialect of the fifth to fourth century BC. Plato uses it unflinchingly, with precision and regularity. The tragic and comic poets, on the other hand, employ it in weird, incompatible ways (not surprisingly, since the difference between tragedy and comedy has less to do with content and more to do with each genre's stance toward the human world). Thucydides avoids it; the waywardness of the dual didn't suit the straight line of historical time. Orators used it, though with great restraint; the number doesn't quite conform to the clarity that political speeches demand.

With the advent of Koine, the dual gradually fell out of use everywhere, with the exception, perhaps, of some dialects in the countryside. It ultimately became a forgotten part of the language.

The revival of the dual during the Imperial Age, by a group of writers known as Atticists, as part of a plan to resurrect the then centuries-old pure Attic dialect—the remnants of a language that, once again, wasn't their own—was nothing more than a lark that had no impact whatsoever on Greek history. The entire Greek world had by then pitted the singular against the plural. The one against the many. One plus one equals two—no exceptions. Same as today.

One of the most original definitions of dual number that I've ever heard came from a high-school student in Livorno whom I used to tutor in Greek. "The dual," she said, "is that thing that you never find in the readings, so you forget it as soon as you've studied it. Then one day, one totally depressing day, it pops up on a quiz, and it's so punishing that you never forget it again."

There's no denying it: you *almost* never encounter the dual in your reading assignments. How likely you are to encounter it depends on whether you're studying Attic-Ionic Greek, the dialect of Plato and Pericles. The dual is preserved most coherently and frequently in the language of Athens, the Parthenon, and the Acropolis.

Further, the totally linguistic, not mathematical, nature of the dual contributes to this *almost*. There is no guarantee that a text that mentions two objects or people will refer to them in the dual form. The dual is never a given, not even in a text about anatomy, where all anyone talks about are eyes, ears, hands, and feet. Whether or not the grammatical number is used depends on the sensibility of the author.

Here's my totally personal definition of the dual: one plus one does not equal two, but *one formed by two*. The Greek word for "two" (δύο) only appears in dual form.

The use of this grammatical number, and all the ambiguities and uncertainties that accompanied it over time and ultimately doomed it to oblivion, were linked to the relationships that an author discerned between two entities. Which is why parts of the body—allied ships cutting across the sea in pursuit of the same enemy, horses drawing the same chariot, twin brothers, spouses, comrades, and divinities—sometimes appear in dual form. And sometimes don't.

My Greek Textbook

The definition of the dual that I have provided comes from page 42 of Γράμματα, the textbook in junior high with which I took my first stumbling steps as a student of the Greek language. Published by Edizioni Cremonese in 1976, the textbook is still assigned in many *licei classici* in Italy.

You can hardly call those first steps a walk in the park. It was more like an uphill climb, as can be seen from the state of my old tome, which has been by my side from Livorno to Sarajevo, survived every move and diploma, followed me from one life to the next. Its cover is wind-battered from all the times I've stuffed the book into my backpack or handbag, and what pages remain are streaked with annotations, a rainbow of highlights, words frantically circled and underlined, the names of ex-boyfriends etched in the margins next to this or that declension, and, above all, the cry of pain—"I hate Greek!"—beside a list of irregular verbs (written in a moment of weakness, it goes without saying, seeing as I was happy and mad enough to major in Classics).

Nor would you call Γράμματα a good read. Like all textbooks, it does its job; it teaches you how to get by, how to tread water and avoid drowning. Its endless black-and-white tables and rules don't make for the most inviting design. It doesn't leave room for giving you a sense of the language. Yet it's a clear reference book that doesn't drone on, and its severe survey of the language even suits it. Whenever something escapes me, I continue to reach for it. In other words, I know that everything there is to know about Greek grammar can be found in its pages. Lastly, the plain heavy paper of Γράμματα is beautiful and now bears the scent of thoughts returned to a thousand times.

Use of the dual depended on the connection between two entities that a speaker did or didn't detect. It is, as I said, a concrete number; a human, not mathematical number. A number that gave meaning to the relationships between objects and people, if there was meaning to be given. An incalculable number that was never imposed by rules of ancient Greek grammar but freely chosen by those who spoke and wrote in that language.

How much do you learn in school about dual number and this way of giving the world a numerical meaning? One sentence. In all of the beginners' textbooks that I consulted and that—at this very moment, as I'm writing this and you're reading it—millennials are sweating over in order to learn a two-thousand-year-old language, only a single sentence is devoted to the dual. Or half a sentence. One that appears in some mystifying spot on a page right before dozens and dozens of charts for memorizing declinations and conjugations.

That sentence almost invariably goes like this: "There are three grammatical numbers in Greek: singular, dual, and plural. The dual indicates two entities (objects or people) that naturally form a single unit, at least according to the author who uses it." That's it. Which must be why students immediately forget the existence of such a mean-ingful number, why it is barely a blip on their linguistic radars (most of us lack this sense of a twinned unit in language).

In other words, you should be grateful to that one quiz where you'll stumble upon the dual, pay dearly for having forgotten about it, and then wave bye-bye (as my young student would say before apologizing to me, to Greek grammar, to everyone up to the Byzantines—as if she were to blame). But it's all too easy to play the blame game and point the finger at the lack of attention that the dual is paid in school: I'd go so far as to call that child's play, without the fun.

Paradoxically, in Italian schools, students constantly study the dual *forms* of all nouns and verbs, meticulously declining and conjugating them in the singular, dual, and plural. There are two declinations of nouns in the dual, one for nominative, accusative, and vocative, and the other for genitive and dative. For example, in the first declination you have τὰ μοῖρα ("the two destinies"), ταῖν μοίραιν ("of/to two destinies"). There are also two verb endings, second and third person dual. For example, in the indicative they are identical: στέλλετον ("you two send"), στέλλετον ("those two send"). What becomes apparent is that the dual is so easy to remember that it's even easier to forget. Usually, you've forgotten it as soon as you've turned the page. Filed it away. I did the same in school, memorizing a little, relying on my ear a little, taking my chances, praying I'd never come across it again.

While writing this chapter, I've paused several times to ask myself why schools teach the dual of every word if the form is so rarely used, so ambiguous, so personal, so unclassifiable.

I spent a long time musing on the meaning of dual in order to talk about it here. (Advanced textbooks devote two whole sentences to this grammatical category of ancient Greek—two instead of one!) The dual always seemed to elude me, as erratic in my mind as it is in Homer's poems. In fact, in the process of writing, I realized that I'd never really understood the dual. I had always written it off as a rare, eccentric, illogical form that evaded all attempts at normalization, and therefore all answers. I had always thought of it as ancient Greek's uncanny grammatical way of counting: singular, dual, plural. I had always thought that, should I come across it on a test, the rules I had learned would be sufficient for deciphering it and applying to it a meaning.

Most of all, I had believed that grammatical numbers in Greek were one, two, and three or more. I was wrong. Dead wrong.

The dual makes sense only because ancient Greek felt the need to put into words something beyond numbers, something that we, too busy making linguistic calculations with the abacus of life, have lost: the meaning of the relationships between things and between people.

Having finally understood the loose, free-standing meaning of this number, it wasn't hard to see why, in school, students study the dual number for every Greek word.

We study it "just in case." We study it as a precaution or provision in the lucky—or unlucky—chance that an author might choose the dual to express the relationship between two eyes, two oxen, two islands, two bodies of water, two friends two sisters, two winds—the relationship between any two things. Which is to say that you study the dual in school *just in case* you happen to encounter it *by chance*.

As a result, today almost no one gets the meaning of the dual—that most ancient, original, and spontaneous byproduct of Indo-European—languishing as it does in a single sentence in a grammar book. Just as with our contemporary modes of communicating via slide, text message, and tweet, in linguistics the economic principle wins every time. Where multiple forms with the same meaning exist, the simplest, fastest, most immediate one prevails.

The same thing must have happened with the dual in ancient Greek. Its sense of twinship vanished, and it was folded into the generic plural form. Considered pointless, the form was abandoned, then forgotten.

Anyone who has had the rare privilege of being truly in love can appreciate the difference, in terms of intensity and mutual respect, between thinking "the two of us" and thinking "we." Yet they have no way of expressing what they think and feel. To do so, they would need the dual of ancient Greek.

Cases, Or an Orderly Anarchy of Words

> Wet from the world
> the scrapped taboos—
> and all the bordercrossings between them,
> pursuing
> meaning, fleeing
> meaning.
> —Paul Celan
> (trans. by Nikolai Popov and Heather McHugh)[10]

Inflected, from the Latin *flectere*, "to bend or curve." Meaning, "to change direction." Therein lies the inner workings of words in the inflected language that is ancient Greek. Free words, whose meanings constantly modulate as they are inflected, whose meanings continually evolve, from one case to the next, as they are declined.

Greek case leaves absolutely nothing to chance: it is a special syntactic category of the language. Cases are the *various* forms that a noun takes to express *various* grammatical functions in a sentence. That is what makes Greek an inflected language: the syntactic role of words is entrusted to changing, or *bending*, their case endings.

---

[10] Paul Celan, *Glottal Stop: 101 Poems*, trans. by H. McHugh and N. Popov (Middletown, CT: Wesleyan University Press, 2000).

The case system and compression of Greek, which contains all it has to say in its word endings, may strike us as complex and ambiguous; every time we face a Greek noun, we have to pause to consider its last, miniscule syllable in order to understand what the word really means. Yet the Greeks chose this case system chiefly for its simplicity and clarity. From that last syllable they could glean both the function and meaning of a word in any given discourse.

Greek inflection and the Greek case system come from Proto-Indo-European, a language not only inflected and synthetic but also agglutinative. From Latin *ad* ("to") and *gluten* ("glue") meaning "to glue, unite, adhere." In other words, "to attach one thing to another."

Proto-Indo-European was a complex, highly synthetic language that used words to their fullest, that brimmed with meaning. Not only was the syntactic function of words entrusted to cases, but the words themselves were formed by attaching to them prefixes, suffixes, and other words. Ancient Greek retains that characteristic in its use of morphemes before words, such as ἀπό ("from"), ἐν ("in"), ἐπί ("against/ toward"), πρό ("before/in front of"), περί ("around"), which can change their meaning. Sometimes a lot.

Proto-Indo-European had eight cases, eight different forms of the same word to express different functions. They were the nominative, vocative, accusative, genitive, dative, locative, instrumental, and ablative. Most of these cases had a semantic value: the nominative indicated the subject of a clause, the genitive possession, the dative the indirect object,

All the Languages in the World

Long after the descendants of Noah were, according to the Old Testament, punished for attempting to defy the heavens by building the tower of Babel, today there are approximately 4,500 different languages spoken in the world, and that number shoots up to 20,000 if you take into account special and extinct languages. In short, Babylon left a big linguistic mess in its wake.

From the point of view of typology, languages are classified as inflected, where meaning is conveyed by the changes to word endings. Inflected languages include Greek, German, and Latin, with its *lupus* ("the wolf") and *luporum* ("some wolves").

Then there are agglutinative languages, like Hungarian and Turkish, where a root word conveys its basic meaning and can be modified by a series of morphemes. The Aztec word *nokalimes*, "my houses," is formed by joining *no* ("my") + *kali* ("house") + *mes* (plural).

On the other end of the spectrum are isolating languages, where every word is fixed and has an independent meaning. The value of a word depends exclusively on its position in a phrase. For example, in Chinese we have *wǒ ài tā, dànshi tā bù ài wǒ,* ("I to love she but she not to love I") which might be translated as "I love her, but she doesn't love me back."

Finally, there are incorporating languages, where a whole phrase or sentence is contained in one extremely long word, like the Eskimo word *angyaghllangyugtuq*: "He wants to buy a big boat." Who knows how many misunderstandings are avoided that way.

and so forth. Three cases had a purely practical value: the locative indicated one's present location, the ablative the place one came from, and the instrumental the means by which one did something.

All Indo-European languages, over time, reduced the number of cases. Still, no language ever chose to reduce, to synthesize as much as Greek. Later languages, like Slavic and ancient and modern Armenian, actually chose to conserve more. Latin still had six cases.

When a case is lost, and its functions are transferred to another case, it is called syncretism. In Greek, the ablative merged with the genitive, and the locative and instrumental merged with the dative, leaving just five cases. Here they are:

• **The nominative case**, ὀνομαστικὴ πτῶσις, names things. As its Greek definition makes clear, the nominative is the case for "calling," or denominating. It was used to indicate abstract or concrete concepts, objects, people, words: ἡ μοῖρα for "destiny" and ὁ καρπός for "fruit." Its most important function is to indicate the subject of a clause, whether the subject performs the action or is acted upon.

• **The genitive case**, γενικὴ πτῶσις, distinguishes between things. It indicates belonging, thanks to the preposition "of" that appears before the noun it modifies and erects a fence around that noun's meaning. That is why the genitive is the case of possession, limitation, partition. More often than not, it is translated with a possessive phrase, τὸ θέατρον τῆς κώμης, "the theater *of the village*."

In Greek, the genitive is also commonly used to express the idea of being a part of something else, something larger, or else a smaller portion of the subject being talked about, separating out and selecting: πολλοὶ τῶν ἡγεμόνων, "many of the generals."

The case can also express belonging (ἡ ἀγορὰ τῶν Ἀθηναίων, "the agora of the Athenians"); jurisdiction (ἐστι τοῦ πολίτου, "it's the job of the citizen"); quality or material (ἡ κόμη χρυσοῦ "hair of gold").

The genitive also denotes value and price (ἡ ἀξία τῆς μιᾶς δραχμῆς, "the value of the drachma"), size and length (ἡ ὁδὸς τεττάρων σταδίων, "the street is four stades long"), and origin (ὁ ἄνθρωπος τοῦ γένεος, "a man of local stock").

To all of these functions of the genitive, properly defined, we can add the functions of the Proto-Indo-European ablative: generally speaking, the concept of derivation or provenance. So that in Greek the genitive expresses the source of movement, the object of an agent, and a subject preceded by specific prepositions.

• **The dative case**, δοτικὴ πτῶσις, indicates where things go.

It indicates the indirect object of a verb, the object toward which an action is directed or which the verb bumps up against. The original value, from which it gets its name, is connected to the idea of *giving* and, by extension, expresses for whom or what an action is done. It is most commonly rendered in English with the preposition "for" or "to": τῇ στρατιᾷ, "for the military."

To these grammatical values of the dative, we can add the values of two extremely concrete cases of Proto-Indo-European: the locative and instrumental cases.

So, depending on the preposition, it can express place (τῇ νήσῳ, "on the island"), time (τῇ ἡμέρᾳ, "by day"), as well as the means, mode, company, and efficient cause.

Finally, the Greeks thought up a highly particular construction for this case, called the dative of possession, which combines the verb "to be" with the person who "possesses" in the dative (and who would become the subject were we to translate the construction). This form exists in Latin and is called *sum pro habeo*, literally, "I am instead of I have."

Therefore, εἰσιν μοι δύο παῖδες, "me two children," would be in the dative in Greek, and we would translate it as "I have two sons."

• **The accusative case**, αἰτιατικὴ πτῶσις, indicates things as they travel toward their destination.

Just as the nominative indicates the subject, the accusative indicates the direct object of a clause, completing the meaning of a sentence and answering the question "Who?" or "What?" Τὴν ναῦνν, "the ship."

In Greek, it originally signified forward movement, movement toward a place, an end, a time, a person.

Therefore, the concepts of moving toward a place (τὰς Δελφιάς, "to Delphi"), of continuous time (τὴν νύκτα, "during the night"), and of movement through a place (τὴν ἀτραπόν, "on the trail") are put in the accusative.

• **The vocative case**, κλητικὴ πτῶσις, is used to call attention to something. Commonly preceded by ὦ, or "Oh!", the vocative is a direct address—spoken out loud—to a person or an entity in the form of a plea, a prayer, a question, an answer, an order, a statement. Or it might simply be used to call out to someone affectionately, as when a child says, ὦ μῆτερ—"Mom!"

In Latin, the arrangement of words within a clause or sentence is called *ordo verborum*, word order.

Capable of indicating the exact function of words without ambiguities, the ancient Greek case system makes for a formidable[11] spectacle: word order doesn't follow a logical pattern but an expressive and, therefore, personal pattern. In Greek, word order is free, absolute, not hemmed in by rules of syntax. Sure, words of secondary importance almost always come after main words, and words whose meanings are connected can almost always be found next to one another. Yet a writer may choose to separate words whose meanings are linked in order to achieve a particular effect.

Generally speaking, in ancient Greek there exist relatively predictable ways of regrouping various cases of words

---

[11] "Formidable," from Latin *formido*, "fear," "fright," is one of my favorite words. Like other peculiar words, formidable is a *vox media*—a word whose original meaning has been lost and that now has two opposite, though correct, meanings: good/bad, positive/negative. It's up to the speaker or the translator to choose which meaning of the vox media is intended—and that's a huge responsibility for language to place on us. "Formidable" can mean either something frighteningly terrible or terrifyingly beautiful. The word alone gives me the chills.

The Latin word *fortuna*, "chance," can mean good luck and rotten luck; *tempestas*, "storm," can be used to refer to weather in general or to a violent tempest; a *monstrum*, or "monster," describes something that is either so beautiful or so hideous that it makes your jaw drop.

Some ancient Greek *voces mediae* are ὁ αἴτιος, "responsible for" something good *or* bad. It can even mean "guilty of." ὁ κίνδυνος means "an event, an adventure," and often (for those of us who cower before our fate) "misfortune." The verb πάσχειν, "to get an impression," can mean "to enjoy" just as often as "to suffer." And finally, the noun ἡ ἐλπίς, "expectation," hovers between "hope" and "anxiety" (as anyone who has ever had to wait can tell you!).

within a clause. But Greek never imposes one rule for positioning words to the exclusion of all other positions.

More importantly, no particular order is used to express a syntactical function: every Greek word that we read is found where it is—and not elsewhere—because the author intended it that way. The purpose of its position totally depends on the individual authors and their choice is totally unrepeatable. That is because of the special way that the Greek languages uses cases. An orderly anarchy of words. A freedom of expression—unbound by essentially syntactical or logical functions—without equal. In no other inflected language—not in Latin, not in Sanskrit—is word order freer, and therefore more personal, than it is in ancient Greek. Thanks to this exceptional freedom, Greek literature gained the flexibility and dramatic—meaning living, genuine—qualities that so seduce us (or fill us with dread) while reading the works of its great writers. Think of a densely-packed dialogue in Plato, the tension conveyed by the chorus in one of Sophocles' tragedies, the pangs of love encapsulated in a line of Sappho.

To recap: ancient Greek is a language with multiple cases and millions of anomalies that preserved the most intimate essence of Proto-Indo-European; its inflection is so rich, so filled with meaning as to endow every word with autonomy, no matter where it sits in a clause. In Greek, there is absolute freedom; every word placed next to another word has an expressive, stylistic value that speaks. Because the order in which the declined words are arranged in a clause is also a means by which the language speaks to us, says something to us—we who are forced to write, speak, and therefore think in a specific, fixed *ordo verborum* that is fundamental to understanding one another and making ourselves understood.

Clearly, our language has lost most of its case endings but not "cases," not the syntactic roles of words within a clause. In the sentence, "the bookseller praises the boy," "the bookseller" is the subject, "praises" is the verb, and "boy" is the direct object. If the sentence were rearranged to read, "the boy praises the bookseller," "boy" would become the subject, "praises" remain the verb, and "bookseller" become the object.

Thanks to the case system, if you wanted to say the same sentence in Greek, "the bookseller praises the boy," the syntactic relationship between the subject and object would remain the same. The words could be written, ὁ βιβλιοπώλης ἐπαινεῖ τὸν νεανίαν. Or, ἐπαινεῖ τὸν νεανίαν ὁ βιβλιοπώλης. Or else, τὸν νεανίαν ὁ βιβλιοπώλης ἐπαινεῖ. Whatever the order, the meaning of the sentence doesn't change, because in Greek, the syntactic functions of subject and direct object are expressed by the inflection of the nominative and accusative, not by their position within the sentence.

To understand the mechanics of Greek, we might borrow the mathematical rule of commutative property (fingers-crossed I don't muddy the waters, seeing as math isn't the strong suit of Classics majors!). Just as in addition, when you rearrange the order of the numbers, the answer stays the same ($2 + 3 = 5$ and $3 + 2 = 5$!), so too the order of words in a Greek clause, which can be rearranged without changing the answer (i.e., the meaning).

But that doesn't hold true in English: The function of words is expressed by syntax, by what side of the verb the words fall. Let's go a step further and add another element to our sentence. Let's say that "the bookseller praises the boy's wisdom." In this case, "wisdom" is the direct object and "boy's" is the possessive noun, while "praise" is the verb and "bookseller" is the subject. Once again, in an English sentence, the meaning is governed by the order of the words. "Wisdom" is the "boy's."

One of the many various freewheeling ways that the sentence "the bookseller praises the boy's wisdom" can be expressed in ancient Greek is ὁ βιβλιοπώλης τὴν τοῦ νεανίου σωφροσύνην ἐπαινεῖ. Here, the verb appears at the end of the sentence, the subject at the beginning, the direct object in the middle, and the possessive noun "the boy's" (τοῦ νεανίου) is actually nestled inside the noun that it modifies (τὴν σωφροσύνην). This is an example of what is sometimes called a bridge, a type of Greek word construction essential for navigating translations: the embedded word refers to the words on either side of it, creating, via the articles and suffixes, an internal connection that resembles a bridge of meaning.

One night, on the cusp of spring, I was in a bar in Milan with a close friend, a whiz at life (not Greek). It was a decidedly happy occasion: we were clinking glasses of champagne, toasting each other's successes. When I broke the news about this book, he turned pale. Just the sound of the word "Greek" killed my friend's mood; he became wracked with guilt and felt compelled to confess that, back in high

Word Taboo

There are some things that you really can't say out loud, and I'm not talking about making up excuses to avoid taking tests at school. I'm talking about word taboo.

Taboo is a Polynesian word that refers to all that is sacred and therefore off-limits. The term taboo commonly refers to anything prohibited from the social sphere (prohibited from being done *and* from being talked about).

By word taboo is meant the ban on using words that refer to taboo objects or people. They can include animals, plants, behaviors, and deeds that a society holds sacred, treats with reverence, or is deeply embarrassed by—and has serious, irrational fears about—and cannot bring up in conversation. The words are substituted with euphemisms (from the Greek word εὐφημέω, "words of good omen," as opposed to "words of bad omen") or by paraphrasis (from the Greek word περιφράζω, "to say in other words").

Given their entirely social nature, word taboos vary from one society to another and from one historical period to another. Just think of all the words pertaining to human sexuality that couldn't be uttered fifty years ago!

A few examples? In Arabic, leprosy is called "a blessed illness" and a blind person "a man with keen vision." The Latins called a deathbed a *lectus vitalis*, or "bed of life."

The history behind labeling some words taboo is really weird.

The city of Benevento in Samnium (in present-day Campania) was originally called Maleventum, "bad wind," because of its strong currents.

---

school, he had skipped an oral exam on the third declension. Only thirty years had passed, but owing to some weird time warp, in the mind of a former Classics student it felt like yesterday. He was a wreck. He hung his head and told me that, like a war deserter, he'd managed to get out of taking the test on cases he was so afraid of by pretending to be sick—for an entire year. In the end, by some strange—

When the Romans conquered it in 268 BC, they changed the name to Beneventum, or "good wind," to ward off bad luck.

A light wind was called *malacia* in Latin, from the Greek word, ἡ μαλακία, "calm, weak wind." Yet when the original meaning faded, people came to believe that malacia was derived from *malus*, or "bad," and thanks to maritime superstition, the wind became known as *bonus*, or "good." Hence the fair winds that blow through all Romance languages.

In some societies certain words are completely verboten. The Greenlandic Inuit can't say the word ice. Australian Aborigines can't speak the name of a dead person. In China, you can't even write the name of the emperor; you have to substitute it with other characters.

One of the weirdest examples are the Germanic and Slavic words for bear. The animal so terrified people that they couldn't even utter the word, for fear that it might leap out of the forest upon hearing its own name, upon being *called*. That explains the German word "Bär" and the English word "bear": both words mean "gray" and refer to the coat of the animal who shall not be named. In Slavic languages and Russian, the word for "bear" is *medved*, literally "honey eater." Apparently, they're hoping that the bear is vegan and won't maul human beings.

And what is there to say about politically correct expressions like curves (instead of plus-size), downsizing (instead of firing), and collateral damage (as if pretending not to *see*, and therefore not to *say*, the murder of civilians during military operations)?

and famous among our *liceo classico* cohort—combination of prayers, pleas, vows, and promises to his teacher, he passed the year with impunity.

Obviously, to console my friend and yank him out of his skeleton-filled closet—or from under his high-school desk—I offered him another glass of champagne, and the haunting memory of that exam faded. But the next morning, a little after sunup, I received a text. "Andrea, I've been up all night. The point is I never really understood this whole business about Greek cases."

Given the impossibility of establishing an automatic connection between a single case and a single definition, it's totally natural and human to feel bewildered by the Greek case system: we always lose heart when we're not sure we've got something down cold. I say natural because Greek isn't our language and never will be. We hear and articulate the world differently from the Greeks, and because of that we are always forced to brood over it as we shuttle between their language and our own.

Teaching Greek, I have come to realize how much eludes us, how much we forget about our native tongue. An ironclad understanding of our own grammar, logic, and syntax is fundamental for learning Greek—for learning any language. How can we even begin to understand in Greek, say, what a complement clause or subjunctive verb is if we don't even know how they function in our own language? Very often we don't know our own language, so forget about knowing another—dead or alive. How many times in my years as a Greekling have I heard myself say, "I don't even know what that means in my own language!"

The fact is, to study a language as synthetic as Greek, a language that says so much with so little, it takes an understanding of morphology, grammar, and syntax that we can hardly expect from someone aged fourteen (or twenty or thirty or forty for that matter!). So, to take on or take up the challenge of the Greek case system, it's more important that we have a good grammar book handy than a Greek dictionary, since you won't find anything there if you don't know what you're looking for in the first place. Now that we're clear that nothing—not one thing—will spare us from having to think through ancient Greek logically, here are some useful instructions for navigating the case system.

First, it's important to keep semantics in mind, what words actually mean, to scan intuitively for the right definition. A passage about war, for example, will likely talk about soldiers, strategies, encampments, and military tactics; on the other hand, in a text about the sea, we'll find terms like prow, mast, rowers, and unfurled sails.

To understand Greek and its case system, we must never get distracted, must never overlook a single word.

Unlike Latin, which has no articles to help guide a translator, in Greek the article and its position with respect to a noun are excellent partners for a translator to find their way through the Greek case system and its free-floating word order. (So much for those who say Latin's easier than Greek.)

Pronouns, those stand-ins for nouns, are also faithful companions on the hunt for the overall meaning of a sentence, because they must always refer to someone or something.

A verb of motion is likely to be accompanied by a place in which the movement is being done. If it is a motion away from ("from Athens"), it will appear in the genitive. If a motion within ("in Athens"), it will be put in the dative. If a motion toward, it will be put in the accusative ("to Athens").

You don't need to be a philologist to tackle doubts and uncertainties. Greek is already speaking to us, albeit in its own way. When you're not sure which complement is called for, just remember the basic idea at the heart of each case, and from there gauge its nature—on a case-by-case basis!—as it applies to the word that you're translating and making your own. The nominative is always the case of saying, of the main subject. The genitive indicates initial movement with a generic and protean "of" or "from." The dative expresses giving, with the preposition "to," or being located, "in." The accusative is a finger pointing toward the object being talked about. As one of my Greekling friends once said, laughing, "Give me a world that's more dative and less accusative!"

Having lost the society that acted as a compass and gave it a vocabulary and voice, every Indo-European language has shrunk its case system to the point of burying cases altogether.

Beginning in the age of Koine, Greek inflection, too, underwent a process of simplifying and reducing the number of its cases among its speakers (not just Greeks but also speakers who belonged to an empire as vast as its Hellenistic counterpart). Starting in the third century BC, many words began to sound strange and difficult, and the irregularity of cases so severe as to appear wrong. The cases were therefore "corrected" by being shoehorned into the simplest possible model: the standard male λόγος. Which is why we have a simpler nominative singular form, γέροντα ("old man"), which is derived from the accusative γέροντα, instead of the classic but now incomprehensible γέρων.

Moreover, in a process that can be detected in nearly every language from Medieval Latin to modern languages, the function of cases has been gradually supplanted by the increasingly frequent recourse to prepositions. For example, in Classical Greek the verb πείθομαι ("to believe in, to have faith in") was followed by the dative. Later, the preposition ἐπί ("to") was tacked on in order to facilitate understanding. And by the outset of the Middle Ages, the dative case disappeared altogether.

The existence of a sophisticated literary language, and the most robust cultural tradition then known in the world, kept hidden—or held back—the evolution of Greek from written texts, and therefore from its speakers. The Greeks could not have been all that aware of the changes to the language that they used every day, the very changes that today we struggle to piece together, that we squint to see in the rearview mirror.

Almost every Indo-European language demonstrates how the final syllables of words were trimmed down over the centuries to the point of vanishing from the various new languages that emerged. The Latin number *unum* becomes *un* in French, *uno* in Italian and Spanish, *um* in Portuguese. Yet ancient Greek, as we've seen, possessed an accent all its own, which prohibited speakers from truncating—from breaking up—words. As a consequence, ancient Greek grammar left no trace of its process of simplification, since it kept almost all of its final syllables.

This resistance on the part of the language mostly depends on pronunciation, and the Greeks continue to articulate words the same way, without contracting the

Greek Colors

"How differently the Greeks saw the natural world. Their eyes, we must admit, were blind to blue and green; they saw dark brown instead of blue, green instead of yellow. They used the same term to describe brown hair, cornflower, and the southern sea, the same term for the color of the greenest plants and human skin, the same term for honey and yellow resin. That is why their greatest painters only painted the world in black, white, red, and yellow. How differently and how much closer to humankind must nature have looked to them, since in their eyes the coloration of humankind also preponderated in nature, and nature was swimming, so to speak, in the atmosphere of human colors!" That's Nietzsche, in aphorism 426 of *Daybreak*, sizing up the chromatic quirks of the ancient Greeks.

In his *Theory of Colors*, Goethe remarks on the extraordinary Greek vocabulary for colors, how it stretches the norms—as different from our own as the Greek language is to our language. The Greeks' associations with colors were so unprecedented that eighteenth and nineteenth century scholars speculated that they didn't even see colors—as if! Of course they saw them. They just had other ways of expressing them. Rest assured, people's eyes have always been and always will be the same.

For the Greeks, color was *life* and *light*, a human experience rather than a physical or optical one. Far removed from Newton's color spectrum theory.

In the *Iliad* and the *Odyssey*, Homer names just four colors: milk white, blood red, the black of the sea, and the yellow-green of honey and wheat.

The words black (μέλας) and white (λευκός) indicated darkness and light (the Latin word *lux* has the same etymology of the Greek color). Colors are in fact created, according to the Greeks, by the play of light and shadow.

In Greek, the word ξανθός signifies a color ranging from yellow to red to green: call it verdigris. It is the warm shade of ripe wheat, as well as the blond hair of all those heroes in Homer and the reddish hue of the fire at night or the round orange sun at dusk.

The adjective πορφύρεος means "agitated, in continuous movement, boiling over" and also stands for Tyrian purple, a color that ranges from blood red to just this side of blue. Πορφυρεύς means "purpura shell fishermen," because the dye was extracted from shellfish and produced by expert dyers.

Cyan (κυάνεος) means blue in general and is applied to everything from azure to dark red to the black associated with death.

Still, my favorite Greek color is glaucous (γλαυκός). Its primary meaning is "bright, gleaming," and it is used to describe the play of light on the sea. Athena's eyes are glaucous, "bright as an owl's," cerulean, blue, bluish-gray.

The illustrious Homer scholar and British statesman William Gladstone was among the first to insist on the luminous impression of Greek colors. In the decades after him, scholars noted the linguistic "quirks" other civilizations used to map colors, including the language of the Bible, and there was a controversial debate among academics over whether the ancients had an underdeveloped sense of color. *Physiologically*—at the level of the retina. Some went so far as to claim that all Greeks were color blind.

But first Darwin's theories and later on studies in physiology and medicine proved beyond a doubt that the opposite was true: the Greeks saw the sea, the fields, the sky, the landscape just as we see them today. Perhaps the colors they saw were more splendid, since they felt the need to express them in another, private way.

The ancient Greeks assigned extra meanings to every color, a sense of luminosity, a degree of clarity. They saw the light and gave its intensity color. The sky is never just blue but vast, bronze, and star-strewn. The eyes are never just blue or gray but glaucous and gleaming.

final vowels. In modern Greek, the word φίλος ("friend") can be found exactly as it was in ancient Greek, every letter intact—no additions, no subtractions. Whereas the French, Italians, and Spanish realized as early as the tenth century that, having dropped the final Latinate syllables, their words had so evolved that they had become different, distinct languages.

On the other hand, Greek grammar developed continuously, silently, *internally*. There were never any ruptures or revolutions. Even its case system survived. Modern Greek (Νέα Ελληνικά) still has four cases: the nominative, the genitive (rarely used in plural form), the accusative, and the vocative. All but the dative are left. On account of this continuity, which includes conservation of the language's complex declination system—unique among modern languages—the Greeks were not aware of the transformation taking place from ancient to modern Greek.

In conclusion, thanks to the case system and its loose word order, Greek, whether ancient or modern, is a language which thinks when spoken, and thinks also when written. Always.

A MOOD CALLED DESIRE: THE OPTATIVE

> If you will tell me why the fen
> appears impassable, I then
> will tell you why I think that I
> can get across it if I try.
> —MARIANNE MOORE, from "I May, I Might, I Must"

Desire. In French *désir*, in Spanish *deseo*, in Portuguese *desejo*. From Latin *desiderium*, from the phrase *de + sidere*, "from the stars." To gaze at some attractive person or thing as if gazing at the hieroglyphic stars at night.

Estrangement, which is to say, turning away, looking elsewhere. The stars fade from view. Longing. Then, in your mind's eye, gazing at someone or something you cannot have, someone or something you yearn for. Hence desire.

In ancient Greek, this business is spoken in the optative mood, as in this fragment from Archilochus:

> Εἰ γὰρ ὡς ἐμοὶ γένοιτο χεῖρα Νεοβούλης θιγεῖν
> καὶ πεσεῖν δρήστην ἐπ᾽ ἀσκὸν κἀπὶ γαστρὶ γαστέρα
> προσβαλεῖν μηρούς τε μηροῖς.

Would that I might thus touch Neoboule on her Hand

[...] and to fall upon her wineskin that works for
hire
and to thrust belly against belly, thighs against thighs.[12]

Ancient Greek conceived of reality, and represented it
in language, in a manner totally different from our own,
taking great pains to choose grammatical mood. In Italian,
the degree to which something is feasible (and therefore
desired) is completely independent of mood. Instead, that
degree is expressed with adverbs and locutions: lots of
words to say or not say where things stand. Maybe too
many. On the other hand, in ancient Greek, every human
action was measured by its degree of potential, by how
likely it was to become reality: for each degree, a speaker
chose a specific mood. A verb in the indicative always indicated objectivity, no matter its position in a sentence; a verb
in the subjunctive or optative mood indicated expectation
or possibility. Ἀναβιῴην νῦν πάλιν, writes Aristophanes in
Frogs. "I'd sooner live again!"[13]

In ancient Greek, only the speaker can take the measure of life, only the speaker is free to choose the verbal
mood by which to represent it to themselves and others.
Is it real, concrete, objective life, or probable, subjective,

[12] Archilochus, Semonides, Hipponax, *Greek Iambic Poetry:
From the Seventh to the Fifth Centuries BC.*, ed. and trans. Douglas E.
Gerber, Loeb Classical Library 259 (Cambridge, MA: Harvard Uni-
versity Press, 1999), Fragments 118, 199, 158–159.

[13] Aristophanes, *Frogs. Assemblywomen. Wealth*, ed. and trans.
Jeffrey Henderson, Loeb Classical Library 180 (Cambridge, MA:
Harvard University Press, 2002), 44–45.

a maybe? Possible or impossible? Is their desire attainable or unattainable?

The following table shows the degrees of reality by which ancient Greek evaluated life events; it will enable us to comprehend how Greeks arrived at such evaluations by their choice of verbal mood. For us to understand, we will have to swim below the surface, like deep-sea explorers, and bring to light the meaning in our own language; for this reason, the example used is all about the sea.

Unreality is the opposite of reality, yet also identical to it. That which has never been or never will be has the same degree of objective and impartial existence as that which was or will be. Both of these *objective* perceptions were expressed in the indicative, on no uncertain terms. "I want to sail," the first and last sentence in the table, can be either realistic or unrealistic; in English, there is no linguistic difference to show what the speaker thinks the degree of likelihood is. The words, whether written or spoken, are exactly the same. Whether the speaker raises anchor or not depends on what they are willing to admit to themselves, on how capable they are of taking a good long look in the mirror; that is how an action becomes possible or impossible.

Our language has no way of distinguishing between an action's likelihood or unlikelihood when it comes to expressing a desire. Period. It's all up to us as we face the mirror in the morning, and how true we are to our word (if you catch my drift, great, and if not, oh well).

Between reality and unreality, there are two degrees

Degrees of Reality

REALITY	**Objective**	"I would like to sail" / "I intend to sail"
PROBABILITY	**Subjective**	"I would like to sail"/ "I might go sailing"
POSSIBILITY	**Subjective**	"I would like to sail" / "I might go sailing"
UNREALITY	**Objective**	"I would like to sail" / "I would have liked to sail"

of subjective reality, which closely rely on how the person speaking sees the world and articulates it: probability and possibility.

Probability means that there is a concrete possibility that an action will be performed, and in ancient Greek that is expressed in the subjunctive. In English, we use the conditional to cover probable reality; the conditional comes from the Latin phrase *conditio sine qua non*, the prerequisite, the point of departure, if something is actually going to get done. That is why the second sentence in the table, "I would like to sail," means that everything's all set and that an action will most likely be performed. We just need to wait for a favorable wind, unfurl the sails, and raise anchor.

Possibility, on the other hand, is a speaker's projection, in words, of their desires, their plans, their fears, even

THE INGENIOUS LANGUAGE · 117

My boat is docked, I'm ready to set sail.	Indicative Mood
My boat is docked. If the winds were favorable, I'd set sail. Let's hope for better weather tomorrow.	Subjunctive Mood
My boat is docked, but I don't know how to sail. I have to train, work up the courage, take a chance, wait for the right winds. Then I'll depart. My boat sure looks pretty in the wharf, but that's not what it's made for.	Optative Mood
I don't have a boat, I get seasick, I live in the mountains, and I don't have plans to make a big change in my life. It's a lost cause.	Indicative Mood

their passion. In Greek, possibility was expressed in the most personal and intimate mood: the volitive optative. Translating it can be complicated, thorny, uncomfortable, since we have to take other people's desires into consideration. The third statement in the table, "I would like to sail," describes a speaker's desire, the likelihood of which depends neither on the right wind nor the cargo onboard. Instead, it expresses the odds that a person must reckon with as they see their desire reflected in the sea and take stock of their courage and their strength: will they raise anchor, leave everything behind, and set sail? Or will they be seized by fear and stay put?

The line between a probable and impossible wish is razor thin, totally dependent on the speaker's sense of responsibility and the action their words translate to.

Whether a desired action will go from possible to probable and become reality, or else slip away into unreality, is—in life as in Greek—all contained in the optative mood.

The word *optative* comes from the Latin verb *optare*, meaning "to desire, wish for, hope." Given its etymology, this exclusively Greek mood is also called the desiderative mood.

Like all incomparably elegant relics, the optative comes down to Greek from the Indo-Europeans. But unlike other languages that are derived from Proto-Indo-European, Greek (as well as the languages of India and Persia) chose to preserve the distinction between the indicative, subjunctive, and optative moods, the infinitive and imperative.

There is evidence that the optative was used to express both desire and regret as far back as Homer's day, though it didn't always draw a distinction between probability and improbability:

> Εἴθε οἱ αὐτῷ
> Ζεὺς ἀγαθὸν τελέσειεν, ὅ τι φρεσὶν ᾗσι μενοινᾷ.
> May Zeus fulfill for him some good, whatsoever he desires in his heart.[14]

No author of antiquity, from Plato to Thucydides and from Sophocles to Aristophanes, is afraid to use the optative to express a desire that might come true, whereas the

———

[14] Homer, *Odyssey, Volume I: Book 2*, vv. 33–34, trans. A. T. Murray, rev. George E. Dimock, Loeb Classical Library 104 (Cambridge, MA: Harvard University Press, 1919), 48–49.

historic tenses of the indicative indicated desires that would never come true.

In short, the optative enables Greek writers to make very fine points of distinction; there is no other mood like it in the world. There are two poles and two colors in the Greek language: real and unreal, black and white. In between, there's the whole color spectrum of human choice.

As a desire fades from reality to unreality it can also be expressed in Greek by various ways of formulating hypotheses. This is the so-called hypothetical period or if-clause, which is formed by a protasis (from Greek προτείνω, "to put forward, propose"), meaning the condition needs to realize what is expressed in the main clause, and by apodosis (from Greek ἀποδίδωμι, "to render or give back").

Reality is put in the present indicative, and probability in present subjunctive. Whereas possibility is put in the past optative, and unreality in the past indicative.

No, linguistically evaluating the degree of realism in human affairs is not left to luck, fortune, destiny, your horoscope, or, worse, chance. Ancient Greek is far more sophisticated than that. Let me be clear: If the odds of something happening are good, Greek uses the subjunctive. If they are not, it uses the optative.

Probability and linguistic decisions are determined by the will of the speaker and external circumstances.

If you say "the libeccio wind might be coming" while standing at night on the Terrazza Mascagni, Livorno's waterfront, and the wind that "ruffles the soul" is, as usual, blowing, then the chances of that happening are excellent.

In ancient Greek you would employ the subjunctive. If you said the same thing on a barren northern heath, the chances of such an occurrence are far more remote, and therefore sorely regretted and sorely desired. In ancient Greek you would employ the optative. But if the libeccio wind was already blowing, the wind would be a reality, so the statement would be made in the present indicative. Were we in the desert, the odds of the wind that "borrows the sound of the sea" arriving would be impossible, the words unreal, and therefore in Greek you would put it in the past indicative.

> Εἴθ᾽ ὣς ἡβώοιμι βίη τέ μοι ἔμπεδος εἴη,
> ὡς ὅθ᾽ ὑπὸ Τροίην λόχον ἤγομεν ἀρτύναντες.

Would that I were young and my strength firm as when we made ready our ambush, and led it beneath the walls of Troy.[15]

That's Odysseus, in Book XIV of *The Odyssey*, opting for the optative, and the nature of his desire, his staggering sense of longing, and his tenacity born of struggle are all wrapped up in the mood of the verb.

In the same book, we meet Eumaeus, the faithful swineherd whom Odysseus loves like a son. After finally reaching Ithaca, exhausted from all his trials, Odysseus learns from his slave that everyone believes the king died at Troy, and

---

[15] Homer, *Odyssey, Volume II: Book 14*, trans. A. T. Murray, rev. George E. Dimock, Loeb Classical Library 105 (Cambridge, MA: Harvard University Press, 1919), 70–71.

that a group of usurpers, the suitors, are vying for his estate and his wife Penelope. Odysseus wants to rally the strength and bravado he felt twenty years earlier at the walls of Troy, but the long journey and the many trials he's suffered have left scars on his body and soul. When Eumaeus asks his real identity, Odysseus lies, passing himself off as a beggar from Crete. Finally, the two divvy up dinner, and poor Eumaeus gives his king, whom he fails to recognize, a cloak to keep warm at night.

Without this context, we'd never fully understand Odysseus' words. They'd be like a declaration of love graffitied on a train station wall—maybe those words still meant something, maybe they didn't. But we know the nature of Odysseus' desire and the urgency with which he has called on the gods to make his long trip home from Troy. (We know this, because we've read the *Odyssey*.)

If we knew nothing of Odysseus' adventures around the Mediterranean, the sentence "Would that I were young" would tell us nothing about his desire to reclaim his birthright and expel the usurpers from Ithaca. All it might convey is an old surge of regret spoken by a man disappointed with his life, an anonymous veteran of the Trojan War.

Nothing would suggest to us that his desire is a *possibility* about to become a *reality*. After ten years to and ten years fro, Odysseus has finally returned to Ithaca and is posing as a refugee to take back his kingdom and wife: to take back his livelihood.

Interpreting what the Greek says by the mood alone totally depends on the sensibility of the translator, who is saddled with the job of deciphering how people's desires are given voice in Greek. To convey the optative in most other languages, more words are called for, or fewer. The difference is one of form, not content.

The optative in this sentence might be teased out in English with expressions like, "I really wish I were young again" or "If only I were as young as I was when we declared war on Troy!" And anything else needed to transmit Odysseus' desire to bring an end to his return (his νόστος) and take his place on Ithaca's throne next to his wife Penelope and his son Telemachus.

καὶ μὴν εἴς γε ἀνδρείαν Ἔρωτι "οὐδ' Ἄρης, ἀλλ' Ἔρως Ἄρη, Ἀφροδίτης, ὡς λόγος· κρείττων δὲ ὁ ἔχων τοῦ ἐχομένου· τοῦ δ' ἀνδρειοτάτου τῶν ἄλλων κρατῶν πάντων ἂν ἀνδρειότατος εἴη.

And observe how in valour "not even the God of War withstands" Love; for we hear, not of Love caught by Ares, but of Ares caught by Love—of Aphrodite. The captor is stronger than the caught; and as he controls what is braver than any other, he must be bravest of all.[16]

If only the meaning of the optative were clearest of all, I'd add!

This is a punishment unique to the study of dead languages: in ancient Greek, the most intimate mood, the mood created to convey desire, elicits further dismay when translating it. I was always well aware that moods

---

[16] Plato, *Symposium*, 196, pp. 156–157.

were taught but almost never explained. Saying Greek has four finite moods—indicative, imperative, subjunctive, and optative—and displaying a chart isn't enough to convey the meaning of the language. Especially if that language has a mindset that our own lacks. Especially if that language possesses something extra that, in our own language, is missing. Especially if that language is beautiful; and ancient Greek is awesome to behold.

Maybe it's my firm belief that in this life—and not just in school—there is value in cultivating a Latin-style *curiositas* (which is a far cry from Italian-style cravings for rumor and innuendo). The desire to discover yourself and the world, to always, like a child, ask why. The need to question everything that doesn't quite make sense, everything that seems weird or bizarre. The beautiful effort to inquire after subjects, languages, human beings, life itself. That's how you learn, in my opinion.

Maybe it's that I have traveled a lot, lived for a long time in different, far-flung places, and have come to learn that you cannot fully inhabit the world, that you will be doomed to pass through it like a tourist, unless you probe the underlying reasons for things.

That's it. The lack of curiosity that I observe in students of ancient Greek, due to certain teaching methods, fills me with consternation. Sometimes even rage. Because no one should spend years studying a language and still feel like a nomad bouncing from rules of grammar to dictionary definitions to a handful of pages in a workbook. Either you inhabit ancient Greek, and really get inside the language, or you remain silent.

Nostos

The word to describe one of the most devastating human desires may look like it comes from Greek, but in all actuality it doesn't. *Nostalgia* is formed by combining the Greek words νόστος, "return," and ἄλγος, "pain, sadness," to express the downhearted wish to get back home, to the place of your childhood, to the people and objects dearest to you. But the word is totally alien to the Greek world. It was coined in 1688 by Johannes Hofer, a medical student from Alsace, whose graduate thesis at the University of Basel was entitled "Dissertatio Medica de Nostalgia." For years the young physician studied the emotional distress of Swiss mercenaries who served Louis XIV, the King of France, were forced to spend many years far from the mountains and valleys of their homeland, and often suffered from an undefined illness that proved fatal unless they were returned home.

Ever since, the Greek neologism *nostalgia* has permeated other European languages, expressing the feeling of sadness and separation

---

How is it that no one, and I mean no one, asks why ancient Greek has this extra mood called the optative and no other language does? How is it that everyone, and I mean everyone, considers it a B-list subjunctive or an alternative version of the conditional? Most of my students have nothing more than a vague idea of the concept of possibility that the optative carries with it. I myself found it vague until I scratched below the surface and took possession of its meaning.

I've often heard it said that the optative is the mood that goes "-oi," on account of its vowel stems—and clearly "oh" isn't your typical cry for joy, nor does it contain a scrap of lexical semantics. Almost always, when handed a text to from the land one loves, a type of melancholy called *mal du pays* in French and *Heimweh* in German. German also has a beautiful word that my language doesn't—beautiful for those who can relate to this strange form of grief. *Fernweh*, a word combining "pain" and "distance," means wanderlust, the desire to go places you have never been.

The *Nostoi* (Νόστοι, "returns") is the title of a group of Greek epic poems about the repatriation of Achaean heroes after the Trojan War. Its author's identity is shrouded in mystery. Some say the author is Eumelos of Corinth, others Agias of Troezen. Preceded by the *Cypria*, the *Aethiopis*, the *Little Illiad*, and the *Illiupersis*, and followed by the *Telegony*, the *Nostoi* is part of the Epic Cycle, a collection of epic poems that tell the story of the Trojan War and are independent of the *Iliad* and the *Odyssey*, which are never mentioned in the Epic Cycle. The latter represents an alternative history to the one that Homer gives us.

translate, the nervous student scans the page like a seagull, glimpses the particle ἄν, and immediately senses a threat, a challenge, hard work ahead. In short, a gigantic neon sign goes on: *Danger!* But for a Greek, the particle actually helps underscore the meaning of the verbal mood: ἄν is none other than a welcome glimmer of the subtleties of significance. Paired with the historic tenses of the indicative, ἄν indicates unreality or impossibility: the action wasn't performed, and it won't be. Paired with the subjunctive and the optative, ἄν indicates probability or possibility: the action is about to occur or may occur. So how do we translate it? Usually we don't. Or rather, we find other ways of rendering the nuance of ἄν in your own language. This time the possibilities are up to us.

So, without freaking out, handling it with all the care it demands, like a box of diamonds marked "Fragile," let's take a look at the meaning of the optative in ancient Greek:

• **The volitive optative**, its original value.

Ποιοίην: "I want to write poetry!" / "For heaven's sake, if only I could write poetry!"

In the sentence above, the optative expresses a desire, a good (or bad) omen, an intention, a helpful piece of advice, a concession—like εἴεν, "let it be," "very well." The desire may refer to the present, the future or the past; you *can* desire for something to have happened in the past (it's called *regret*).

The verb can be preceded by the particles εἰ, γάρ, εἴθε, ὡς to mean "if only," "I sure hope."

The negative is μή— after all, there are some things we don't desire.

• The **potential optative**, or possibility.

Ἄν ποιοίην: "I may write poetry" / "I could write poetry."

The potential optative expresses the likelihood of an event coming to pass or not, as well as an invitation, a prayer, a polite command, or an ironic ἄν λέγοις, "by all means," or οὐκ ἄν φθάνοις λέγων, "go on, the suspense is killing me!" (said with a wink and a smile).

It could be translated with auxiliary verbs to form a conditional or, better yet, with a circumlocution with the verb "to be" that enlarges the meaning of the phrase. In many languages, the conditional retains a sense of irony, say, "I *might* have plans" (when you want to skip another dreary brunch, if only to get back at that ugly word), or, "If it were anybody else, I *would* ask . . ." (when you want to sugarcoat a steep price).

The negative is οὐ—after all, there's a lot of wasted potential.

• The **oblique optative**, or the lens through which the speaker views the world.

Ἔλεγεν ὅτι ποιοίη: "He said that he was writing poetry" / "He said that he wrote poetry."

Frequently used in storytelling, the oblique optative appears in all kinds of subordinate clauses (final, causal, temporal, declarative, etc.) supported by a main clause in the past tense. In this instance, the optative loses its original meaning and preserves only a hazy sense of possibility. It indicates indirect (i.e., oblique) speech. You might say that it underscores a degree of *subjective* distance between the speaker and what is being said about them. Once again, it's a question of courtesy, accuracy, integrity.

Using the oblique optative is not obligatory; it is determined by the person talking about other people's thoughts and actions—the liberties they take, and their sincerity. If only the media (or what little remains of it) had this Greek mood!

Poetry

The word poetry comes from the verb ποιέω, "to make, do." The verb also means "to build, construct," as in *by hand*. For the Greeks, there was nothing poetic about writing poetry, at least as we tend to think of it. It was a job like any other, the same as carpentry, masonry, or pottery. Except what got made was poetry.

Poetry was born a few centuries after Homer and Hesiod, when the Muses clammed up, quit dictating from Helicon, and forced the Greeks to invent a new genre with which to describe their world in verse.

Homer and Hesiod made epics, not poetry. Which is to say, they adopted meter to tell stories (Ἔπος). In the seventh century BC, the world changed. We went from a universal culture, which suited the epic's ability to encompass everything about being Greek, about an "us," to a culture of individuals, which demanded stories about the feelings, passions, grief, and moods of an "I."

There were two main genres of Greek poetry, monodic (for soloists) and choral (for choruses), and two main subjects, gods and men.

Each genre had its own dialect. Choral poetry was written in Doric, monody in Aeolic. That's the Greeks for you: they tend to file everything into neat categories. When the poet opened their mouth and out came Doric, listeners knew what to expect from their verses. It didn't matter if the poet was born in Sparta or on Lesbos. The choice of dialect was a poetic—meaning practical—choice, made to be understood.

And the poets?

The scholars of Alexandria, who decided what we should read—not that we ever asked them to—by creating a canon, passed down to us nine poets almost intact: Alcaeus, Anacreon, Alcman, Bacchylides, Ibycus, Pindar, Sappho, Simonides, and Stesichorus. All we have of all the other poets are just fragments, "fallen leaves, windblown," as the heartbreaking Mimnermus would have put it.

And how did the Greek poets fare economically? Like craftsmen.

Today, if your family's wealthy, you can amuse yourself making whatever kind of tables and chairs you're into, like Archilocus, who says that if the battle takes a bad turn, he'd willingly give up his shield; he'd rather save his own skin. Or, like Sappho, you're lovesick. Or, like Alcaeus, you sing about being a raging alcoholic.

But if you're poor, you make the chairs that your benefactors tell you to, as Pindar did. Some poets sang at weddings for money. Back then, some poets wrote on commission. Dario Del Corno, author of a popular guide to Greek literature, calls Pindar an occasional poet. Pindar did write occasional poetry, and he was the most famous and brilliant practitioner in the field. Give him a couple of dates, names, and cities, and he could mold anybody into a hero or demigod and reach back ten generations to exhume their mythological roots. In short, he was a total professional when it came to occasional poetry. And there was never any shortage of occasions for him. Pindar mainly wrote in honor of the winners of Panhellenic games, the oldest sports festivals in the world. (Besides the famous Olympics, there were the Pythian, Nemean, and Isthmian games).

Why was Pindar hailed as the high priest of poetic purity but his occasional poetry and particular profession ignored?

I have my own personal theory about this: because, despite the indisputable beauty of every word, no one understood a thing he wrote. What are Pindar's most famous flights of fancy if not the lines we least understand? I've never met anybody who really got Pindar. Voltaire, who shares my opinion, once wrote, "Pindar, whom everyone praises and no one comprehends."

To give you an example, and to dispel any doubts a reader may have by letting them judge for themselves (I'm not trashing Pindar, whom I love despite not understanding him), here is "The Nemean Ode II," for Timodemus of Acharnae, winner of the pankration.

> *Just as the sons of Homer, those singers*
> *of verses stitched together,*
> *most often begin with a prelude to Zeus,*
> *so has this man received his first installment of victory*
> *in the sacred games at the much-hymned*
> *sanctuary of Nemean Zeus.*

But Timonoös' son is still indebted—if indeed his life,
while guiding him straight on the path of his fathers,
has given him as an adornment for great Athens—
to pluck again and again the fairest prize
of the Isthmian festivals and to be victorious
in the Pythian games; and it is likely

that Orion is traveling not far behind
the mountain Pleiades.[17]
And indeed Salamis is certainly capable of rearing
a fighter. At Troy Hector heard
from Ajax; but you, O Timodemus, the stout-hearted
strength of the pancratium exalts.

Acharnae is famous of old
for brave men, and in all that pertains to athletic games
the Timodemidae are proclaimed foremost.
From the games beside lofty-ruling Parnassus
they have carried off four victories,
whereas by the men of Corinth

in the valleys of noble Pelops
they have so far been joined to eight crowns;
there are seven at Nemea in Zeus' contest, and at home
too many to count. Celebrate him, O citizens,
in honor of Timodemus upon his glorious return,
and lead off with a sweetly melodious voice.[18]

[17] A Pindarian flight of fancy. —AM

[18] Pindar, *Nemeans Odes*, ed. and trans. H. Race, Loeb Classical Library 485 (Cambridge, MA: Harvard University Press, 1997)

The survival of the optative in Greek, the one Indo-European language to safeguard it tenaciously, is proof of Greek's unmistakable, extraordinarily durable verb system. Verbs, not nouns, dominate ancient Greek. Through aspect and mood, Greek verbs indicate ideas from the point of view of their process, their development, and the way a speaker perceives them. They don't express mere things but the actions from which those things spring into being.

All Greek dialects from antiquity make clear distinctions between the subjunctive and optative, between probability and possibility.

But during the first century AD, the optative was gradually being eclipsed. The verbal mood was already experiencing a crisis and being swapped for simpler words like "maybe" and "perhaps." And all crises, linguistic or otherwise, get worse; the nuance that the optative encapsulates couldn't withstand the implosion of dialects into one single imperial language, Koine. For one, the verbal mood rarely appears in the Greek translation of the New Testament; you can find a few examples in later scrolls, but it is always employed in vows and prayers. In any case, that is the optative in little more than survival mode, and we can picture it languidly slipping away from the free, normal language that the Greeks chose to speak. All evidence points to the optative's having first been dropped from phrases in which it was used to express possibility, then from subordinate oblique clauses; the last written examples of the optative are prayers to divinities. Desire, yes, but of the religious variety.

If Roman authors like Strabo, Polybius, or Diodorus

Siculus rarely used the optative (compared with Plato and Xenophon), it must have been even more rarely used in casual contexts.

In short, the subtleties of the optative were too delicate to endure for long without becoming confused and diminished, without losing intensity. Modern Greek only has the subjunctive. The optative has vanished for good.

No current language bears a trace of the optative. That stands to reason, since in Latin only a hint of it, the orphaned relics of its meaning, survives in the subjunctive, which is derived from an ancient desiderative form (*sit*, "let there be," *velit*, "want to").

The story of every modern language demonstrates how the optative and subjunctive couldn't inhabit the same space for long; the line separating them was both too thin and too thick. Therefore, the distinction between the subjunctive and optative was variously and independently erased from all Indo-European languages. From the outset, it was clear that sooner or later the optative would be the one to perish. The subjunctive has been spared because many subordinating clauses in Latin, as in Italian and French, call for it; it is seldom used in main clauses. Though it expressed certain nuances, as a verbal form the optative was not essential to understanding and making yourself understood. It embodied a graceful way of expressing your desires and coming to terms with your life (and words) without imposing your will on others or overwhelming their lives (and words).

About the disappearance of this verbal mood, the incomparable Antoine Meillet once remarked, "The loss of the optative reflects a decline in Greek refinement; it's the loss of an aristocratic elegance."

For that matter, every language is democratic, a "social fact" subject to the whims of time and how those who speak it see the world. Whatever you might say in the age of Twitter and WhatsApp, people change before the language changes, not the other way around. Every word of every language is exposed to the democratic use it is put to by those who speak it; like a sculpture, it is exposed to the winds of democracy, which continue to worry away at its contours.

Medea, one of Euripides' most harrowing tragedies, begins with a nurse lamenting what she may have been and never became—with a desire that can no longer be fulfilled. Life has taken a different course. Instead, the Argo has landed, and everything has already happened.

> Εἴθ᾽ ὤφελ᾽ Ἀργοῦς μὴ διαπτάσθαι σκάφος
> Κόλχων ἐς αἶαν κυανέας Συμπληγάδας,
> μηδ᾽ ἐν νάπαισι Πηλίου πεσεῖν ποτε
> τμηθεῖσα πεύκη, μηδ᾽ ἐρετμῶσαι χέρας
> ἀνδρῶν ἀριστέων οἳ τὸ πάγχρυσον δέρος
> Πελίᾳ μετῆλθον. Οὐ γὰρ ἂν δέσποιν᾽ ἐμὴ
> Μήδεια πύργους γῆς ἔπλευσ᾽ Ἰωλκίας
> ἔρωτι θυμὸν ἐκπλαγεῖσ᾽ Ἰάσονος.

Would that the Argo had never winged its way to the land of Colchis through the dark blue Symplegades! Would that pine trees had never been felled in the glens of Mount Pelion and furnished oars for the hands of the heroes who at Pelias' command set forth in quest of the Golden Fleece! For then my lady Medea would not have sailed to the towers of Iolcus.[19]

The Greek optative is, for this reason, the perfect measure of the distance between the effort required to take stock of what we desire and the strength needed to express it—to ourselves most of all; in the conviction that, no matter the situation, elegance is what gives us a slight but sure advantage, especially when it comes to language.

It's just us—and our desires.

[19] Euripides, *Cyclops. Alcestis. Medea*, ed. and trans. David Kovacs, Loeb Classical Library 12 (Cambridge, MA: Harvard University Press, 1994), 284–285.

So, How Do You Translate That?

> I prefer to arrive at speech
> from silence. To handle a word
> with care, so that, like a boat,
> it slips gently toward the shore,
> and the wake of my thoughts traces its figure.
> Writing is a peaceful death;
> the brightened world expands
> and an edge of it burns forever.
> —VALERIO MAGRELLI, from *Ora Serrata Retinae*

Right, so, how do you translate Greek? What does that even mean? How is it done? These are the kinds of questions I get most often from the kids I teach Greek. Wouldn't you know, they're the same questions that I used to ask the teacher when I was a student.

Questions like these may be centuries, if not millennia, old, and took root at the exact moment that we stopped understanding, and making ourselves understood in, ancient Greek, so that translation has become the one way to understand it. (For some reason, in *licei classici*, we refer to translation with the obsolete term "version.") Further proof, the latest confirmation—as if we needed any—of the death of classical languages. All foreign languages get translated; Latin and Greek get "turned."

"Version" comes from the Latin verb *vertere*, meaning "to turn, alter, change" and, therefore, "to translate." *Verti tiam multa de Graecis*, "I have often translated from the Greek poets as well," Cicero tell us in *Tusculan Disputations*. To translate comes from the Latin verb *traducer*, meaning "to transfer, expose, lead across or over." Meaning, to carry from one place to another.

To carry the signified over the barrier of the signifier—that is the main purpose of translation, no matter the language. A translation will never be the same as the original work; it is a path toward that work's original meaning. The result is an uncanny encounter, like bumping into a stranger who is somehow immediately familiar. Even if no one speaks it anymore, ancient Greek has the same effect on us.

When we translate, we inch toward the meaning of a language that is and always will be different from our own. Translation is a journey toward a language with particular qualities, qualities that make it special, which we cannot sense because we lack the language skills to do so, and therefore must translate, must light out for other places—and other ways of saying them.

To reach the end of a journey—and who can say where the journey leads?—requires a perfect understanding of the language; that much is indisputable. Read: study, sweat, toil, tenacity.

But also fundamental is an ear for sensing what the language is telling us, from a past that, though remote, has not completely dissipated. Why study the language if its meaning were lost entirely?

Translation calls for fluency, consistency, and trust in ourselves and the language. A text *speaks*; we just need to listen. (And, no, I didn't hallucinate or swoon as I stared at a translation assignment at 8 A.M. and was forced to choose to either kill or be killed by Greek. I understood then that the only way to proceed was to think like the Greeks. That has been my method for over fifteen years, and it is my first, most important piece of advice for undertaking a translation (or, if you prefer, version).

When staring at a Greek text, a translation student's first reaction ranges from terror to fear to panic. Fifty shades of anguish. Anyone who has ever studied Greek knows this. Those who haven't probably have similar anxiety stories about mathematical equations, diagrams, chemical nomenclature. But with all due respect, that's just anxiety. Not the sheer bewilderment that anyone who studies Greek experiences, at least once in their lives, upon being given a passage to translate. The paralyzing fear of not understanding. The horror of looking at mysterious scrawls on handouts and not having the foggiest clue as to what they mean. And for some reason, the handouts are always badly printed, so blurry and washed out that they look as if they were photocopied directly from Athenian inscriptions. I remember during one exam staring at the page for over an hour and feeling lightheaded, perhaps because I was hyperventilating from the stifling air in the classroom and the July heat, unable to lift a muscle, not even to open the dictionary. Luckily, I recovered, otherwise I wouldn't be here today to tell you about it.

Greek has been dead for a thousand odd years and it

still continues to make anyone who approaches it freak out. So much so that I've come to think that abject terror is the *sine qua non* of learning Greek.

At forty-three years old, a dear friend of mine had the good fortune (and misfortune) of helping me on this book—I owe him a lot. One evening, throwing up his hands after reading one of my e-mails, he said: "I never got a word of Greek at school. Just receiving your chapters makes me queasy!" So, the fear never goes away, not even when you reach adulthood. Damn.

Many of my students say that translating makes them apprehensive because Greek has a different alphabet. While that's perfectly true, the alphabet is a means of communicating *a* language, not *the* language: all it is is a writing system for getting the sounds of words down on the page. Once we've learned how to decipher it, we're in charge, it's ours. Besides, things could have been worse; at least the Greek alphabet is composed of letters and not, as in Japanese, ideograms, or, as in Linear B, syllables!

Many proceed to tell me that it scares them because the words are different, that they don't resemble their own. What can I say? It's another language—a *foreign* language. Do we find the same words in Spanish? The one way to overcome this fear is time. Experience. Practice. The more often we encounter a Greek word, the more likely it is to get lodged in our brains and become a word of our own.

Learning to translate Greek in school is a race against time, and success is directly proportional to our propensity to pick up the dictionary. The less faith we place in ourselves and language, the more fiercely we cling to the dictionary, like castaways to a raft. True, at the outset we don't know many words of Greek, and having a dictionary is fundamental. True, when doubts and uncertainties arise, the dictionary is a faithful companion. Yet a mad, desperate reliance on the Greek dictionary may turn out to be counterproductive—even dangerous. Counterproductive because every dictionary provides a limited range of definitions (kind of like a stockade of definitions, don't you think?). Moreover, if you're unable to absorb the meaning of even a handful of ancient Greek words, you will keep clinging to your dictionary and retreat further and further from the language, like a castaway who refuses to abandon the raft and trust that the rescue boat is on its way.

The dictionary can, ultimately, be perilous. Students who fly into a panic develop so little confidence in their abilities that they wind up poring over page after page to lookup every definition of a word (and in the meantime that sad, relentless tick-tock of the clock, donated to the school by the local credit union, reminds them that they are running out of time). Students seem unwilling to believe that the definition they're looking for is the first one listed in the dictionary, the simplest and most common definition, and they end up choosing the last, which may turn out to be a bit of slang used by a poet from some remote island who has now been utterly forgotten.

To be clear: given the cost of dictionaries, I'm not suggesting you throw yours out or sell it on eBay. (How many students can't afford to go to a school where the classics are taught? In Italy, I have met untold numbers of students who come from families who struggle to purchase textbooks and dictionaries or pay for private lessons, families who are left to their own devices by the public school system.) What I am suggesting is that we not held be held hostage to the dictionary. That we not check every comma and word just to feel safe (I admit, that's what I did, at least at first). That we trust in what we've learned. Most importantly, that we never think of translation as a mechanical, one-to-one process where A in Greek always equals B in the target language. Were things that simple, then all we'd need was the right dictionary to translate every language in the world. Since the time of Babel, we've known that not to be the case, unless you believe that translation merely entails stacking together a group of words and having Google Translate spit them back.

To translate a text, to best approximate its meaning, sometimes we need to add a word, and sometimes we need to subtract a word, as we move from one language to another. We must always keep our ear out for what the text itself is telling us in order for us to say it in our own language.

"Do you know *every word* in Greek, Ms. Marcolongo?" my stunned students ask, while I stand there equally stunned that, just because I know Greek, they address me as "Ms." and take me for an old woman (the same used to happen even when I was twenty!). No, of course not. I do not know every word in Greek, even if I graduated with honors from a *liceo classico*, hold an honors degree in the

Classics, and have translated many texts; given the wide variety of dialects in ancient Greek, odds are not even a Greek
knew every Greek word.

I still use a dictionary, and frequently. For the sake of
transparency, I'll make it official: I don't even remember
the endless quirks of grammar and syntax, so that I often
consult textbooks—without holding my nose (unlike some
so-called academics, who for whatever reason have wound
up hating their job, themselves, and everyone else).

I once sat for a college exam that required translating
Greek on sight. This is a story I almost always refrain from
telling my students so as not to deal the killshot. The exam
consisted in translating aloud—on the fly, without the
aid of a dictionary, in a few seconds—a passage of Greek
chosen at random by the professor. I repeat: any passage
of Greek fished up from the whole of Greek literature.
Barring the memorization of all of Greek literature, there
was only one way to pass the test: I had to forget about
committing things to memory and apply my fluency and
intuition. No, I can't stand here today and say it was easy.
But it wasn't traumatic either. I was certainly less afraid
than I was facing the "versions" in high school. Because
by then I had studied Greek for ten years and the language
had become mine; sort of.

The exam went swimmingly despite my not knowing
every word in the text that the professor placed in front
of me. It was an unforgettable passage from Lucian about
a man's journey to the moon. All that happened was
what normally happens when you're speaking a foreign

142 - ANDREA MARCOLONGO

Liceo Classico

The *liceo classico* actually predates Italy itself. The first law establishing a public secondary school where Greek and Latin were taught dates back to 1859, two years before Italian unification. Then came the Gentile Reform of 1923. Inspired by the Neo-Idealist philosopher Benedetto Croce, the reform created a five-year program, two years of junior high and three years of *liceo classico*, which has tormented generations of Italians ever since, who sweat bullets at their desks and feel pangs of nostalgia once they've finished their studies.

With six hours a week of Greek, six of Latin, and four of philosophy, the *liceo classico* was, from the start, conceived of as a school for the elite. The textbooks were prohibitively expensive in illiterate and agrarian Italy, a country that had just gotten out of one world war and was about to enter another. And, until 1969, only graduates from the *liceo classico* had access to all Italian universities, while students who attended schools outside of the humanities were barred from studying literature and law.

After over a century of being lambasted as a school for the bourgeoisie (you had to attend it if you wanted to hold political office), the *liceo classico* was put on "trial" in 2014 at the Carignano Theater in Turin. Scientists and economists accused it of being "antiquated" and "behind the times." The inimitable Umberto Eco spoke for the defense. While agreeing that the classical education system needed to be reformed, he argued that there would be no engineers and physicists if they were not humanists first; in other words, if they were not fully sentient human beings.

With the deluge of reforms that began in the 1990s, Italian schools increasingly resembled corporations, with all their point systems and

language and the meaning of one word escapes you, while all the others make sense: you can figure out the meaning of the word you don't know by using your intuition and approximating the original as far as possible. For once you've credits, and the "crisis" of the *liceo classico* in Italy became inexorable. It was considered "pointless" and "too hard," and progressively drained of its original purpose (Latin and Greek were reduced to a few hours a week). In 2019, only 6.7% of Italian students chose to enroll in this type of secondary school as opposed to the myriad schools offering Chinese, drama, and astrophysics.

There's no point in summoning Pericles, as I see it. If it's true that Bill Gates studied the humanities, and Mark Zuckerberg recited Homer at college and Virgil in Facebook boardroom meetings, then that is because, to quote my maestro Italo Calvino, a classic is not that which is "old," but that which "has never finished saying what it has to say."

In one sense, the *liceo classico* is fortunate to be facing a crisis; "crisis" comes from the Greek word κρίνω, "to choose, decide": every day we interrogate our vision of the world and what we want to hand down to our children, who are by no means destined to be Greek scholars—that's for universities to decide.

For my part, I didn't write *The Ingenious Language* to argue that the humanities are superior to the natural sciences. Besides, separating the two was unheard of in antiquity. But after three years of visiting schools around the world, I can affirm what Lila, one of the coprotagonists from Elena Ferrante's novel *My Brilliant Friend*, knows all too well: the one way to gain independence—as an individual and from your social class—is an education. (How many kids have I met who attended *liceo classico* whose families had never studied before? As the daughter of parents who didn't, I'm one of them.) What one gains, toiling away at a grammar book and a translation, is an awareness of being not a Latin expert, but a man or a woman, a citizen of the global world in 2019.

understood the meaning of a sentence, the step toward approximating the meaning of each word is done.

Problems arise when the entire meaning of a text is lost on you. Or should I say, when you fail to read the text in the first place because you're scared of the Greek alphabet or worried about running out of time. So you throw yourself into translating the first word, and then every other word, in the exact order that they appear, whatever that order may be, and then patch them together in your own language, as if they were the colored sides of a Rubik's Cube, and then attach a meaning to the passage (or invent one).

I know that all teachers recommend reading the entire passage before beginning to translate, and that no student ever does. (Not even I did in high school—why lie?) When I asked my students—and myself—about this grand refusal, the answers I got were always the same: I don't understand any of it anyways. It means nothing to me. Reading it is pointless.

Embarking on a translation of a language that you've been studying for one, two, or five years, already convinced that you won't understand a thing and that the text you're staring at is mute, is no way to begin. I see it as a serious breach of respect: respect for ourselves, for the language, and for the time we have spent studying it. But this happens constantly. I've never seen more befuddled looks than when I ask questions like, "What do you remember about ἀρχή (pronounced archē) or γράφειν (pronounced grá-phein)?" But do they not bring the words archaeology and graphic to mind? No, apparently they don't. The alphabet barrier—and, if you ask me, people's natural apprehensions about the language—seem to cloud our view of resemblances between Greek and our own language. And that is how you stop wanting to understand, because you're sure you don't understand.

Socrates' remark, "I know that I know nothing," becomes the alibi and safe haven of every student. May I be so bold as to disagree: You do know it! You know how to read Greek. There's so much you know. So many rules. As you study it, the language becomes your own. The commas, periods, common verbs—they mean absolutely nothing to you? I refuse to believe it.

Have faith in yourself and what you know; it is a matter of respect, really.

Grammar is another cause of blind panic. Before they've even begun to read the text, many students will notice that one or another construction is being used and feel in their heart of hearts that they don't remember the rule or haven't studied it the way they were supposed to, so they wind up desperately abandoning any attempt to understand the rest of the passage.

First, let's get something straight: no text, whether in Greek, Latin, Italian, or French, is merely an accumulation of grammar rules to be solved. This isn't a trivia contest, a math equation, or a rebus. A text exists because the person who wrote it felt the need to express or relay something. And that something certainly isn't a grammar rule that you don't remember.

While translating with my students, I'm often met with definitions of grammar so precise, so beyond reproach— "This is an impersonal verb that refers to blah blah blah" and "It can be rendered in Italian by paraphrasing blah blah blah"—that they would make both a Byzantine monk, and a member of the Linguistic Society of America faint.

Again, I'm not saying there's anything wrong with knowing grammar inside out. Actually, I find it heartening (and I'm envious, since I no longer know it as well as they do). It is wrong, however, to consider knowledge of grammar the end and not the means of translation. Knowing the rules of a language is essential to a basic understanding of the texts written in that language. But a language isn't its rules.

Have you forgotten this or that rule? Don't worry, study harder next time. This time, you might miss something and you won't get 100 percent. Thankfully you've understood what the rest of the Greek passage means and have no need to feel guilty, incompetent, ignorant, or a failure.

Once again, it's a matter of respect. The text has many interesting things to say: dig them up, bring them to the surface, and put them *in your own words*.

Another, not insignificant problem, is age—how much can we expect a young person to know about Greek history, culture, civilization, and politics?

For those of us who are now adults, it is easy to look at young people (and even easier to look at ourselves at that age) and offer a bit of advice, spit out an opinion, encourage them to keep studying, and then cozy up on the couch and get back to reading our books and newspapers, or to listening to our music, whose meanings and language are geared toward adults (or should be, rather; we seem to live in an age when people never grow up, when at forty we're still kids and at forty-one we're all of a sudden old.)

Despite all the efforts by recent textbooks and a few enlightened teachers at schools where the languages and cultures of antiquity are to provide students with a greater understanding of the globality of the Greek world, and not just the Greek language, history programs are not in lockstep with classics programs. And because, in the Italian *liceo* at least, students have to cover the entire history of human civilization (or are supposed to), inevitably only a month or two is devoted to the study of ancient Greece. The same goes for literature, art history, philosophy, and geography (if in fact the last subject is taught at all).

As a consequence, students know very little about ancient Greece—far too little to understand or to not find mystifying the texts that they are asked to translate about military tactics, oracles, religious customs, mythology, and politics; which is not to say that most adults know much about it—I'm positive they don't. How many times have I been asked "What is this about?" when the texts cover subjects that now seem ordinary to me, yet to a young person are understandably obscure.

Besides, when was the last time you heard a student, out at a bar, turn to his friends and say, "Man, I feel like a sword of Damocles is hanging over my head!"? And if he did, would he know the origin of that expression? I seriously doubt it. It stands to reason, then, that students will have very few historical or social reference points to fall back on when reading the story of Damocles or the oracle of Delphi or about how Pericles quelled people's fears during an eclipse. To say nothing of the passages about war, those dozen or so lines taken from the never-ending—and very beautiful—histories of Thucydides or Xenophon, which, according to my own personal survey, students hate most, myself included. The subject is almost always an implied "they" ("they" who? The Athenians? The Greeks? The Persians? The barbarians?) and the object an implied "them" ("them" who? See above). Even when translated perfectly, the passages—a dozen or so lines about encampments, military tactics, armies, sieges, strategies, and sacrifices—always leave us with questions: Who are we talking about? Who won? Who lost? It's a mystery.

Seeing as I dedicate a large portion of this chapter to exposing my students' and friends' fears, I am—alas—morally obligated to turn the spotlight on my own.

Which means I am compelled to tell you about one of my biggest blunders in high school, a blunder so disgraceful that, after a few sleepless weeks, I decided to put it behind me, to never tell anyone about it, to act as if it never happened. Yet it did happen, and I'm going to confess it in order to prove how important it is to have a well-rounded education in the ancient world, in addition to knowing the language and grammar, and being sensitive to language generally. But please, cut me some slack. Don't rub my nose in one of the most traumatic experiences of my high-school career.

It's my final exam in Latin (though it may as well have been Greek) and my first year at the *liceo classico*. Everything is on the line, including my right to spend the summer by the Tyrrhenian Sea, mindlessly frolicking in the sand and swimming with medusae.

The title of the text is written in bold letters, in Italian: "*Il Ratto delle Sabine.*" After that comes the text to translate. I'm fifteen years old and up until now I have been a strong Latin student, so everything's under control—I've got this.

The problem is that I've never heard of these Sabine women. Who were they? What was their deal? As for *ratto*, having grown up in the countryside, I knew exactly what that was: an ugly rodent with a long tail and red eyes.

I presumptuously set about translating, but the meaning of the text didn't add up. By no means did it add up. It appeared to be a jumble of words, a tongue-in-cheek Dadaist experiment. The Sabine women and the rats had nothing to do with one another, apparently. Weird, I thought, very weird. When time was up, I turned in my sheet of paper, miserable and incredulous.

A few days later I was handed back the paper with a nice fat D on top, written in red ink, and I would never have recovered from the trauma of it had I not learned to laugh at my mistakes (come to think of it, it would take another fifteen years, since I have only now learned to laugh at my mistakes).

So, what happened that infamous day at the end of May? No one had ever told me about how Romulus, having established Rome and finding it short on women with whom to populate the city, abducted those living in the surrounding area, including the Sabines. Abduction hadn't even crossed the anteroom of my mind. Acting on the Italian title (and my touching innocence), I never suspected that the Latin word *raptum* had nothing to do with "*ratto*," a rat, but was a participle of the verb *rapto*, meaning "abduction," from which we derive the English word, "rape." So, I had tarnished their memory by mixing those poor women up with rats. Talk about embarrassing!

I hesitate to make excuses, but in my defense, why was the text called *Il ratto delle Sabine*, that is, "The Rape of the Sabine"? Why couldn't they have said *abduction* to avoid confusing a fifteen-year-old whose sweet little mind was already set on the beach? How many living Italians think the word *ratto* means anything other than a rat?

But I was the one to blame. Forgive me. Or take pity on me. I knew almost nothing about the founding of Rome; no one had ever told me the legends of that city when I was fifteen. I was ignorant, in the true sense of the word: I *ignored* things. Still, I beg everyone to forgive me, especially the Sabine women, and I'll keep begging for the rest of my life.

One last note.

In the Italian *liceo classico*, only the work of prose authors is translated, from Plato to Plutarch, Aesop to Xenophon, Thucydides to Aristotle. Each of these writers has his own distinctive, *personal* writing style—just like us. Once again, time, patience, and practice are called for in order to get accustomed to recognizing an author's quirks: all the time it takes to learn to hear the author's *voice* and render it as best we can in our own language. It isn't a question of different forms of Greek; it's a question of different ways of using Greek.

Plato is free to express himself in a completely different mode than Thucydides because he's Plato. Just as Dave Eggers uses American English in a completely different manner than his contemporary Jonathan Franzen, and a book by Orhan Pamuk is beloved, rather than seen as a snooze, if you consider slowness to be a hallmark of Turkish life, and therefore of Turkish writing.

If at school all you translate—or *handle*—is Greek prose, that leaves poetry out altogether. Not just the lyric poetry of Alcaeus, Sappho, and Pindar but every epic, comedy, and tragedy—the heart and soul of Greekness.

"What a relief!" students will say. What a pity, say I; they don't know what they're missing, and most likely never will, seeing as the chances of their enrolling in a classics course in the future are slim to none. Greek poetry is treated as a pure, divine literature to be handled with kid gloves. Sure, translating poetry is ten times harder than translating prose, but it's ten times more meaningful too. Sometimes, usually in upper division courses, you'll translate an entire tragedy, verse by verse, over an entire year. In my case, it was Sophocles' *Oedipus Rex*. It was a laborious undertaking, yet invaluable, so charged with life, that *Oedipus Rex* is one of the tragedies that remains closest to my heart, to say nothing of my mind and my tongue.

There's a big difference between reading an author's work and hearing about an author's life. I could be a proud Livorno native and describe for you the poet Giorgio Caproni, but all you'd be left with is a description, not the beauty of his poems and his person, which are bound up with his poetry. That is why I'm perplexed by the glut of Greek textbooks that talk about poetry and never show any. It deprives the students of one of the most intimate and profound uses of the Greek language. Who cares if it's "tough," the real reason to learn a language is to understand its most complicated visions, not its simplest.

To this day I both smile and shudder to recall my Greek literature textbook from high school, which, while describing the life, death, work, and miracles of every author, also commented on their style. How can you learn about a writing style when you've never read the text and likely never will? It's like providing a detailed description of a painting that no one will ever lay eyes on! I'll never forget my disappointment when I came across the definition of Aeschylus' style as "steep and craggy." Whatever that means, I thought at sixteen and think now, at thirty, and will probably think when I'm eighty. Who knows what is meant by those two adjectives, which I can associate with a hiking trail but not a poet's verse. The only way for me to understand it, and for you to, too, is by reading Aeschylus, and every other author, in their language, if you're brave and lucky enough.

Let's take a close look, in real time, at how translation is done.

I don't have magic formulas or miraculous solutions. Everything you've read up until now are my own, highly personal recommendations, all that I have gathered from my experience over time. Kind of home remedies bearing grandma's stamp of approval, knowledge that has been passed down and patiently accrued over a lifetime.

There is a big difference between dynamic translation and formal translation. Schools almost invariably demand or prefer the latter: utter fidelity to the text, and as a result, the abdication of all freedom. Which is reasonable, of course, as one spends far too little time with one's hands in the Greek language to ever use it for one's own purposes. It's hard enough to express what an author meant to say in Greek, let alone expressing *oneself* in Greek!

What matters, in any case, is the distance between a correct translation and an incorrect translation. A formal translation is all well and good until it becomes a prison, an iron cage that turns Greek into a rusty version of the "target language."

Greek is a concise language, a language that expresses grammatical relations, from cases to verbal constructions, with just one word. In short, Greek feels no compulsion to overexplain: many of its constructions are implicit and impersonal, its meanings captured by a prefix or suffix. It's an almost epigrammatic language, which may account for its having invented the genre.

This is why an overly academic translation chiefly risks producing a text in the target language that is even more obscure and incomprehensible than the original Greek. Leaving participles implicit, infinitives infinite, pronouns literal, certain translations can be so scholarly that they themselves have to be translated. Convincing students to give themselves wiggle room, to loosen up a bit and be less inhibited, is almost impossible; the terror of making a mistake, the fear of taking a chance that may not be to the teacher's liking (as if Greek were a matter of taste!), the anxiety about clarifying something that isn't clear: all these motives compel them to sacrifice meaning on the altar of grammatical convention.

This is how the idea of translation as an act of "carrying something from one place to another" breaks down, and

The Particle

As any student can tell you, Greek texts are overflowing with grammatical particles that are hard to translate. The most common are μέν, δέ, γάρ, and, δή. The reason for their frequency is that Greek did not originally employ punctuation marks (or "interruptions"), as most languages today do. Punctuation marks and accents were added later under the Byzantine Empire to facilitate the understanding of written texts in a language that was growing increasingly Byzantine. Particles abound in Greek texts because they serve the same function as modern-day punctuation. Parsing a sentence depended on them, and therefore they were hugely important, semantically speaking. The problem is that they are very often untranslatable.

Μέν and δέ are without a doubt the most frequently used and most difficult to render. They can almost always be found a few words or clauses apart, and they are logically connected. Generally speaking, μέν introduces the first point of an argument, and δέ introduces the following points attached to the first. These two particles kept a train of thought

the meaning of the translation becomes as mysterious as the original. Instead of blazing a trail, we run in place.

I am perfectly aware that translating dynamically requires the kind of fluency, experience, and confidence that underclassmen rarely possess. But maybe upperclassmen do. We're not talking about "making things up"—as my students say with a shudder—but about getting so close to the language you can touch it.

I have selected the following passage by Xenophon, regularly referred to as "Nothing is achieved without effort." My choice wasn't random. In fact, the passage encapsulates the whole point of this chapter.

on the right track. They are typically used in descriptions, narratives, and treatises. I tell people to omit the copious construction "on the one hand / on the other" unless it is absolutely necessary. Μέν and δέ appear so often that you'd end up having too many "hands" on deck! Given that μέν is pivotal, the primary point, you don't have to translate it (I almost never do). Δέ can be translated as "while" or "instead" or simply with a comma to mark the flow of discourse. If you come across them on their own, μέν usually means "certainly" and δέ retains its sense of a turn or change in direction, which you can simply translate as "but."

The particle γάρ is also ubiquitous. Usually appearing at the beginning of a sentence, as in the passage by Xenophon below, it indicates that an idea previously mentioned is about to be explained. (The problem is that the idea itself is usually missing from the excerpt provided to students, which leads to misunderstandings about what exactly is being talked about.) Γάρ can be translated as "for" or "in fact"; or else omitted.

Lastly, δή adds emphasis and specificity to the word it follows. It can be translated as "exactly" or "really."

To demonstrate the difference, I have taken two approaches to the translation. The first is subserviently academic. The second, though grammatically correct, is totally loose.

Τῶν **γὰρ** ὄντων ἀγαθῶν καὶ καλῶν οὐδὲν ἄνευ πόνου καὶ ἐπιμελείας θεοὶ διδόασιν ἀνθρώποις, ἀλλ᾽ εἴτε τοὺς θεοὺς ἵλεως εἶναί σοι βούλει, θεραπευτέον τοὺς θεούς, εἴτε ὑπὸ φίλων ἐθέλεις ἀγαπᾶσθαι, τοὺς φίλους εὐεργετητέον, εἴτε ὑπό τινος πόλεως ἐπιθυμεῖς τιμᾶσθαι, τὴν πόλιν ὠφελητέον, εἴτε ὑπὸ τῆς Ἑλλάδος πάσης ἀξιοῖς ἐπ᾽ ἀρετῇ θαυμάζεσθαι, τὴν Ἑλλάδα πειρατέον εὖ ποιεῖν, εἴτε γῆν βούλει σοι καρποὺς **ἀφθόνους** φέρειν,

τὴν γῆν θεραπευτέον, εἴτε ἀπὸ βοσκημάτων οἴει δεῖν
πλουτίζεσθαι, τῶν βοσκημάτων ἐπιμελητέον, εἴτε διὰ
πολέμου ὁρμᾷς αὔξεσθαι καὶ βούλει δύνασθαι τούς
τε φίλους ἐλευθεροῦν καὶ τοὺς ἐχθροὺς χειροῦσθαι,
τὰς πολεμικὰς τέχνας αὐτάς τε παρὰ τῶν ἐπισταμένων
μαθητέον καὶ ὅπως αὐταῖς δεῖ χρῆσθαι ἀσκητέον· εἰ δὲ
καὶ τῷ σώματι βούλει δυνατὸς εἶναι, τῇ γνώμῃ ὑπηρετεῖν
ἐθιστέον τὸ σῶμα καὶ γυμναστέον σὺν πόνοις καὶ ἱδρῶτι.
—XENOPHON, *Memorabilia*, 2, 1, 28

Scholarly Translation[20]

The gods in fact do not give anything that is beautiful
or good to men who do not work hard or possess zeal,
but if you want to gain the gods' favor, then you need to
honor the gods; if you want to be loved by your friends,
you must be of help to your friends; if you seek the honor
of a city, then you need to be of service to that city; if you
believe it worthwhile to be admired for your virtue by all
of Greece, then you need to make an effort to do well by
Greece; if you want the earth to produce fruits in abun-
dance, then you need to cultivate the earth; if you think
it right to enrich yourself by way of flocks, then you need
to tend such flocks; if you want to be renowned in military campaigns and if you want to possess the strength to
liberate your friends and subdue your enemies, then you
need to study the martial arts under those with knowledge

---

[20] NB: As these passages illustrate two different translation styles,
their English translations have been made from the author's own
translations from the Greek. —Trans.

of them, and practice their correct use; but if you also want to be strong of body, you need to accustom the body to submit to the mind and train with toil and sweat.

Dynamic Translation

People gain nothing from the gods of beauty or value without hard work and perseverance. If you want the gods to be good to you, honor them. If you want your friends to love you, do well by them. If you want a city to celebrate you, do your best to serve the city well. If you want all of Greece to admire your talents, you must strive to put them to good use. If you want the land to bear lots of fruit, farm it. If you decide to invest in cattle, look after them. If you want to excel in combat, to free your allies and punish your enemies, it is essential to study the techniques of war under someone in command of those techniques, and to train in order to practice them properly. But if you would rather have a sound body, you must let your mind rule your body and train hard with sweat and tears.

Both translations are grammatically correct, irreproachable. No professor could object to them.

But which one speaks to you, to us?

It's funny to observe how four or five years spent translating Greek still affects people ten, twenty, or thirty years after graduating. I'm don't just mean its effect on their grammar but the indelible impression that handling this ancient language leaves on the language of a person who has studied it.

The Takeaway "A": The Alpha Privative

The literal meaning of ἀφθόνους, which appears in Xenophon's passage, is "free from envy." Figuratively, it means "abundant, generous." The adjective is formed by ἀ + φθόνος, or "envy, slander."

Here we see an example of one of the most brilliant quirks of ancient Greek in action: all it takes is a letter, alpha, to take away or negate a word's meaning and turn it into its opposite. This is the so-called alpha privative, from the Greek στερητικός, meaning "that which has a negative quality." No other language before it had employed so simple yet crucial a tool for reversing the meaning of a word.

Tacked on to the beginning of a noun or verb, the vowel alpha completely negates a word's original meaning, transforming it into a completely different noun, verb or, as in the passage by Xenophon, adjective. Thanks

---

I can often recognize those who have studied the classics—and not just by the bifocals they wear. I can recognize them by the way they speak and write: the tell-tale signs that Greek has crept into their way of seeing and describing the world, and never left. Besides a depth of vocabulary—inevitable after spending five years studying word after word after beautiful word—and a certain penchant for hypotaxis—for complicated discourse composed of long subordinate clauses—some habits of Greek speech not only survive but *live on* in those who have studied Greek.

In primis, correlation. Having had to translate texts in which ideas are logically opposed (the Greeks adored counterarguments to reinforce the gravitas of their logic!), a person who slogged through Greek often employs binary phrases packed with "on the one hand / on the other" or "not only / but also," clearly the influence of all those "μέν /

to this feature, in Greek every word can be transformed into its opposite just by adding the letter α, automatically doubling a speaker's vocabulary, creating an endless variety of meanings with which to express (or cancel out and transform) reality. Depending on the case, privative alpha can indicate absence, as in ἀκέφαλος, "headless"; privation, as in ἄπολις, "without a country"; negation, as in ἄβιος, "uninhabitable."

The use of the prefix *a-* or *an-* to suggest privation has survived and prevails in almost all European languages: Italian uses *a-*, of Greek origin, as in *amorale* ("amoral") and *in-*, of Latin origin, as in *incivile* ("uncivil"). But nowadays negative prefixes in Italian are so often associated with specific words, like "analgesic," that they often do not retain their positive meaning. As a consequence, the original power of alpha, the single letter capable of changing or doubling the meaning of nearly every word, has waned.

δέ" and "οὐ μόνον /ἀλλὰ καί" instructions found hundreds of times in Greek texts.

In secundis, the demand for coherent argument. It is extremely unlikely that those who have made every effort to keep up with Plato's ironclad logical deductions will be fooled by a manipulative piece of journalism, a politician's self-contradictory speech, an unsolicited opinion on Facebook, or assembly instructions from IKEA.

Some of us still indulge in etymology. I, for one, can't live without *seeing* that the word "geography" comes from Greek and means "to describe the earth" or that "telephone" means "to call from afar," from the noun φωνή (voice) and φωνάζω (to call).

Others will remember the ancient wars, phalanxes, military tactics, triremes, encampments, barbarians, divinities, and heroes, and imagine themselves as heroes while watching epic American sagas and making fools of themselves in front of their friends.

I have no statistics handy, but I believe that the semicolon has been saved from ultimate extinction thanks to students of Greek. Years of translating the Greek "·" with ";" leave their mark!

Studying ancient Greek has a certain effect on your way of speaking, writing, and thinking—you might call it a strange effect. Even if it isn't cherished in the classroom, the language remains our own, inside us, and rises to the surface in striking and surprising ways.

Ancient Greek, it has long been said, broadens your mind. Not only that, an education in the classics throws the doors open to adulthood.

Through hard work, determination, and the willingness to make sacrifices, people who study Greek learn to recognize and decipher the many facets of life, which is every shade of gray and not just black and white, despite what we might think when we're young, when we're either in love or at war. The satisfaction, pride, frustration, and disappointment that learning this language entails make it easier to manage the joy and heartache of adulthood.

It isn't just a question of linguistics; it is a question of one's attitude toward life. Young people who have had to contend with ideas larger than themselves have a more accurate understanding of the boundaries of hardship and happiness, work and humor, that they will navigate as adults. It doesn't matter whether you are a gifted student of Greek or a hopeless one. By studying the language, you acquire a human skillset that no other discipline—or so I believe—can bestow. Joining a Classics department is like being (unwittingly) cast as a lead in a Greek tragedy or comedy: *there* is where an early, intense sense of being in the world is safeguarded, where you, its students, learn about yourselves, not knowing whether you ought to laugh or cry, whether you have won or lost, whether you are near or far, whether you have truly understood or not.

"I have loved the language for its flexibility," writes Marguerite Yourcenar, "like that of a supple, perfect body, and for the richness of its vocabulary, in which every word bespeaks direct and varied contact with reality. I loved it because almost everything that men have said best has been said in Greek."

Sometimes I think of a Classics department as a prep school for adulthood. Because it is hard, it makes life easier later on. It doesn't matter if you choose to forget Greek or preserve its memory after you've taken your final exam.

I cannot say if studying Greek facilitates one's future academic career, since I continued to study classic literature. Most of my students say it does, even if they have switched to economics or dentistry or another foreign language. One of my students even joined the navy, which made me proud—and a little envious. I am certain, however, that studying Greek helps you develop a talent for life, love, and hard work, for choosing to take responsibility for your successes and failures. It also helps you take pleasure in things, even when things aren't all that perfect.

GREEK AND US: A HISTORY

> . . . from the bridges
> spanning the river I'll discover where
> the seagulls nest, having flown
> this far.
>
> You won't recognize me
> as you turn home without a glance,
> will never know the outcast
> girl who cuts across your path and
> laughs.
> —GIUSEPPE CONTE, from *Poems*

What Is a Language?

A language, any language, is human—every word of it. The life of a language resides neither in the psyche—in the individual thoughts—of those who speak it, nor in their speech organs—the lips, the throat. The life of a language resides in the human beings who use it to comprehend the world, who live by putting that world into words. Therefore, the life of a language resides in society.

A language, as Saussure and Antoine Meillet have argued, is "a social fact," because it expresses a unique world view. Language serves those who share that world view so that they can make themselves understood and be understood. A language cannot exist without men and women who speak and write in that language: if a language has no more human beings who express themselves in it, then it is called a dead language.

At the same time, a language is immanent, independent of any one person. A language doesn't suddenly change because someone comes along and modifies a word. Every linguistic change is a social change first: if the society that speaks that language changes, then the language will change with it.

Linguistics is the scientific study of languages and the changes that take place within them. It is not an exact science. Nor does it belong to the mathematical and natural sciences. It's a social science. Because language is not the sum of its rules, contemporary linguistics intersects with archaeology, anthropology, statistics, social geography, ethnology, economics, and, most of all, sociology.

Language is not engineering: there can be no set of incontrovertible laws that govern how words change, just as there are no ineluctable laws that govern how each human being changes.

Looking back at our language—at the Italian of Petrarch, Ariosto, Manzoni, and Calvino—my fellow Italians often get the impression that a language is simply handed down from one generation to the next (about thirty generations separate Dante's language from our own). This is how we wind up believing that changes to our language—be it a word that disappears or a word that emerges; a final syllable that gets dropped or an initial syllable that gets added;

a verb that is forgotten or a verb that is imported from elsewhere—are merely casualties of this automatic transfer from parent to child, from one mouth to another.

Anyone lucky enough to watch a child learn to talk knows that isn't the case. We don't need an academic institution to tell us that a mistake or a little ad-libbing won't change the way everyone else speaks the language: the most a blip can do is make us smile. Similarly, anyone who has traveled to a foreign country knows what it means to feel marginalized, confused, or disoriented when you don't speak the language of a place: blurting out a word in your own tongue won't change the local language. (Here, too, all it does is make us smile, as when unwitting immigrants in my country say "Thank you" after being told off, and who knows how many times the same thing has happened to us "smart" travelers brandishing our copies of *Lonely Planet*.)

Language is a tool for civilization, the expression of a shared consciousness. Not a tool for a nation; nations come later, with the smooth or crooked lines on the world map, drawn by who knows who for who knows what reason (or maybe that's what wars and religions are for). Statehood alone doesn't account for a common language. Think of all the languages in India. Think of Arabic, which is spoken from Morocco to Iraq, or English, which is spoken everywhere. Are we all English? Dream on.

Geopolitics has nothing to do with language, but human geography does. If national unity is insufficient, cultural unity is, however, necessary for creating a common language.

A language derives meaning from a world view and

the expression, by people, of that view in words. There is perhaps no language that illustrates this truth better than Greek. For millennia, the Greeks were neither a state nor a nation, yet they were always a people. Constantly moved to measure their language against their conception of life, they formed, refined, loved, and rejected Greek, choosing its words over the words of their neighbors and sometimes over their conquerors, century after century, millennium after millennium.

A living language, a dead language: the significance of Greek is encapsulated in the Greek gaze, Greek history, and most of all the Greek mindset.

Indo-European

The pluperfect bellies the truth about Greek: it's an Indo-European language. There is no better term than this to explain—to justify or excuse—the peculiar nature of Greek. It's Indo-European.

But what exactly is meant by an Indo-European language? There is no trace of Proto-Indo-European, nor was it ever written down. Therefore, there are no records of it, and no accounts of the people who used it. Yet the majority of European languages (or rather, all European languages except Basque, Etruscan, Finnish, Hungarian, Iberian, and Turkish) and some Asian languages (Armenian, Iranian, Sanskrit, and the languages spoken in India) are too closely connected for it to be a coincidence. The links between all ancient and modern languages spoken across Europe and Asia prove that they descended from the same prehistoric language. That is to say, from Proto-Indo-European.

With no historical record to go on, we are left to reconstruct it. Our current ideas about Indo-European are the result of linguistic studies aimed at piecing together and deepening our understanding of one of the first languages ever spoken in the world. There were once human beings who, for a time, employed the same pronunciation, the same vocabulary, and the same grammar to define the world: to make themselves understood and be understood.

Yet there have never been two people who have spoken or written in the exact same way. Nor has a language been handed down unchanged from one generation to another. Think about it. Do we speak the same language as our grandmother? Pen the exact same greeting card—or type the same SMS? Think about how much our world has changed—and our words with it—in just fifty years: our technology, our science, our medicine, our politics. Consider how many words we've needed to create in just half a century to talk about objects and ideas that had never been spoken or thought before—that had no etymological precedent! On the other hand, how many words have disappeared because the objects and ideas that they referred to have been forgotten, lost, rendered obsolete, their etymology faded and worn out?

From radio to television, from letters to e-mail to the various devices in the era of social networking, our means of communication also contribute to changing the language.

With Proto-Indo-European, as with all languages, the

same language spoken by the same population transformed over the course of centuries.

But if human beings who share a common language do not sustain their social and cultural bonds, they will no longer be just one race but many different races with different linguistic developments and, ultimately, different languages. Those languages, though derived from the same mother tongue (Proto-Indo-European), will therefore be regarded as distinct, because the people who use them to describe their distinct (and distinctive) societies are distinct. When human beings no longer feel they speak the same language—because they feel they belong to a different civilization—their linguistic differences multiply, and their languages drift apart.

That is exactly what happened to the Romance languages. As new races and civilizations formed after the fall of the Roman Empire, Latin rapidly evolved into French, Italian, Spanish, Romanian, Portuguese, Catalan, and Provençal.

In addition to the Romance languages, the other languages derived from Proto-Indo-European are the Germanic language group—English, German, Dutch, Norwegian, Danish, Icelandic; the Celtic group—Welsh, Breton, Irish; the Indo-Iranian group—Sanskrit, Vedic, Persian, Urdu, the minority languages spoken from Oman to Afghanistan to Pakistan, the Avestan of the Zoroastrian religious texts; and the Balto-Slavic group—Slovenian, Serbian, Bosnian, Bulgarian, Russian, Polish, Belarusian, Ukrainian.

"All the images will disappear," begins Annie Ernaux's

wonderful *The Years*, a novel dedicated to the memory of an entire race.

Today, we struggle to think of ourselves as related, at least linguistically, to those who inhabit the European continent, from East to West. Similarly, during the fifth century BC, the Greeks saw Persians as nothing more than barbarians, and they couldn't understand, let alone recognize, their kinship with the languages and cultures of the Persians and Hittites.

Yet in English we say *father*, in Greek *patír*, in French *père*, in Sanskrit *pitar*, in Gothic *fader*, in Italian *padre* and in German *Vater*. Each of these comes from the same source: the Proto-Indo-European word **pəter*. The words we use to talk about our family and loved ones, like our memories of them, are the slowest to fade. Likewise, we can clearly recognize the Indo-European root **məter* in the English word *mother*, the Italian *madre*, the Sanskrit *matar*, the Greek *métēr*, the French *mère*, the Slavic *mati*.

Yet the roots of words tell us little about the human beings who chose them to express their highly personal world view. We don't even know that world; it is closed off to us forever. All that we do know is that between the fifth and second millennium BC there was a civilization with a common language, and therefore a common society, and over time that civilization branched off into different languages and societies. Archaeologists have brought to light traces of the Bronze Age civilizations in Europe and Asia that must have belonged to the so-called Indo-European civilization. But these weapons, tools, and relics are merely the means for speculating about their history, meaningful scraps that fail to provide us with an image of that brilliant population, much less with the language they spoke every day as time marched on and they were relegated to oblivion. Archaeology is a precious science but mute.

Proto-Indo-European was so widespread because the Indo-Europeans brought with them a uniform, shared, distinctive, and dominant culture. The same is true of English, for example, which remained the language of the United States even after its independence from Great Britain, Spanish and Portuguese in South America, and French in certain parts of Africa.

Proto-Indo-European words—and their ways of describing the world—can be very helpful for pinpointing the geographic origins of the Indo-European civilization. For example, we can look at the names of plants, since plants are easily located: it's nature, after all. According to one hypothesis, the Indo-Europeans had a word for birch tree that can be traced to words with the same root in Sanskrit, Iranian, Slavic, Russian, Lithuanian, Swedish, and German. Birches typically grow in the mountains, in cool, humid climates. There are no birches in Greece, so you won't find the same word in Greek; the people gladly dropped it after settling in an area where the word is totally irrelevant. Such linguistic considerations, along with archaeological and ethnographic studies, have enabled us to place the Indo-Europeans in regions north of the Caspian and Black Sea. At the outset of the fourth millennium BC, there began a long process of migration and settlement of the Eurasian continent.

During this thousand-year-long march from east to

west and north to south, as different civilizations came into contact and different territories were settled, new and different societies emerged, and with them, new and different languages. Among them was Greek, the language spoken by Indo-European peoples who had reached the Greek peninsula and islands around 2000 BC.

Greek Before It Was Greek: Common Greek

Another thing we know about Greek is its ancient history. Common Greek, that is to say, the language out of which all Greek dialects grew, developed around the second millennium BC.

We can't say anything for certain about the era of Indo-Europeans and Greek prehistory. We have no material evidence about the shift from one language to the other, which lasted more than a thousand years. All we have to go on are hypotheses, silent archaeological ruins, and illuminating guesswork.

We know for sure that the word for "sea," θάλαττα, which the soldiers of Xenophon cry out, weeping for joy, when they first catch sight of the Black Sea from the summits of Trabzon, after marching desperately for a year, is neither Greek nor even Indo-European.

> Ἐπεὶ δὲ οἱ πρῶτοι ἐγένοντο ἐπὶ τοῦ ὄρους καὶ κατεῖδον τὴν θάλατταν, κραυγὴ πολλὴ ἐγένετο. Ἀκούσας δὲ ὁ Ξενοφῶν καὶ οἱ ὀπισθοφύλακες ᾠήθησαν ἔμπροσθεν ἄλλους ἐπιτίθεσθαι πολεμίους· εἵποντο γὰρ ὄπισθεν ἐκ τῆς

καιομένης χώρας, καὶ αὐτῶν οἱ ὀπισθοφύλακες ἀπέκτεινάν
τέ τινας καὶ ἐζώγρησαν ἐνέδραν ποιησάμενοι, καὶ γέρρα
ἔλαβον δασειῶν βοῶν ὠμοβόεια ἀμφὶ τὰ εἴκοσιν. Ἐπειδὴ
δὲ βοὴ πλείων τε ἐγίγνετο καὶ ἐγγύτερον καὶ οἱ ἀεὶ ἐπιόντες
ἔθεον δρόμῳ ἐπὶ τοὺς ἀεὶ βοῶντας καὶ πολλῷ μείζων
ἐγίγνετο ἡ βοὴ ὅσῳ δὴ πλείους ἐγίγνοντο, ἐδόκει δὴ
μεῖζόν τι εἶναι τῷ Ξενοφῶντι, καὶ ἀναβὰς ἐφ' ἵππον
καὶ Λύκιον καὶ τοὺς ἱππέας ἀναλαβὼν παρεβοήθει· καὶ
τάχα δὴ ἀκούουσι βοώντων τῶν στρατιωτῶν Θάλαττα
θάλαττα καὶ παρεγγυώντων. Ἔνθα δὴ ἔθεον πάντες καὶ οἱ
ὀπισθοφύλακες, καὶ τὰ ὑποζύγια ἠλαύνετο καὶ οἱ ἵπποι. Ἐπεὶ
δὲ ἀφίκοντο πάντες ἐπὶ τὸ ἄκρον, ἐνταῦθα δὴ περιέβαλλον
ἀλλήλους καὶ στρατηγοὺς καὶ λοχαγοὺς δακρύοντες.

Now as soon as the vanguard got to the top of the
mountain and caught sight of the sea, a great shout went
up. And when Xenophon and the rearguard heard it,
they imagined that other enemies were attacking also
in front; for enemies were also following behind them
from the district that was in flames, and the rearguard
had killed some of them and captured others by setting
an ambush, and had also taken about twenty wicker
shields covered with raw, shaggy ox-hides. But as the
shout kept getting louder and nearer, as the successive
ranks that came up all began to run at full speed toward
the ranks ahead that were one after another joining in
the shout, and as the shout kept growing far louder
as the number of men grew steadily greater, it became
quite clear to Xenophon that here was something of
unusual importance; so he mounted a horse, took with
him Lycius and the cavalry, and pushed ahead to lend

aid; and in a moment they heard the soldiers shouting, "The Sea! The Sea!" and passing the word along. Then all the troops of the rearguard likewise broke into a run, and the pack animals began racing ahead and the horses. And when all had reached the summit, then indeed they fell to embracing one another, and generals and captains as well, with tears in their eyes.[21]

For a period of time, the Greek language had no word for the sea, or else had forgotten it. That proves that the first Indo-Europeans came from mountainous inland regions, far from the coast. Various ancient and modern languages attest to the existence of a common Indo-European root, *mor*. The Latin word *mare* (from which the Italian word *mare*, the French word *mer*, and the Spanish word *mar* are derived) indicates a vast body of water, as opposed to the word *lacus*, meaning a pond or lake. But the Russian word *more* and the Slavic word *mor* signify an enclosed body of stagnant water, like a swamp. Which is to say, the opposite of *mare*. In the majority of Indo-European languages, there is no common root for *mare* whatsoever.

When a portion of the population of Indo-Europeans— by then Greeks—encountered the Mediterranean, they were compelled to come up with new, different names to call it; likewise, their proximity to the sea made them a new and different civilization.

---

[21] Xenophon, *Anabasis*, IV, 7, trans. Carleton L. Brownson, rev. John Dillery, Loeb Classical Library 90 (Cambridge, MA: Harvard University Press, 1998), 21–25.

The Greeks chose to call the sea ἡ ἅλς, "an expanse of saltwater," using the feminine form to distinguish it from the masculine word ὁ ἅλς, "salt." No other language beside Greek uses the word "salt" to refer to the sea; faced with the practical, human need to name something that had never been seen before, maybe the Greeks were as moved by it as the soldiers of Xenophon traveling home to Greece.

Ancient Greek possessed a wide variety of other fascinating words to refer to the sea: Ὁ πόντος, "a passage, path" to elsewhere, as in the navigable sea (the same meaning can be found in the Latin and Italian words for "bridge," *pons* and *ponte*). "Τό πέλαγος, "a broad plain, surface," is of uncertain origin and indicates the wide, flat surface of the sea, like a plain or a blue meadow (again, Latin has *planus*, "plain," and Italian *pelago*, "high sea"). Last, the Greek term to refer to the sea that Xenophon uses, θάλαττα, is also of obscure origin; it may come from one of the unknown groups of people who inhabited the Mediterranean before the Greeks. The term has no precursor or successor in any language in the world except Greek.

All of the Greek dialects known to us that we can now read are derived from Common Greek, a language that had already irreversibly departed from Proto-Indo-European.

Languages transform most rapidly when they become imperial, which is to say, when they become the language of conquerors. We can therefore posit that Common Greek began to change when it became the language of a people that was politically and, more importantly, culturally dominant. But, in the absence of written accounts and historical

174 · ANDREA MARCOLONGO

data, all we can do is speculate about what happened. Once again, digging below the surface of words can help.

Take the case of ὁ νομός, "pasture," and ὁ νόμος, "law," two terms identical save for their accent. Both are derived from the same root, νομ/νεμ, meaning "to distribute." The first, ὁ νομός, means "the portion of land entrusted to the νομάς', or shepherd." It refers to a period of nomadic farming and is the origin of our own word *nomad*. The second, ὁ νόμος, refers to a society that has settled in a specific area where the pastures are designated by law; Greek civilization, and with it the core meanings of its words, had changed.

In modern Greek νόμος still means *law* and νομός *province* or *administrative division*, as in Νομός Θεσσαλονίκης, or the province of Thessaloniki.

Proto-Greek—and subsequently ancient Greek—kept the distinctive, exceptional structures of Proto-Indo-European that bore with it both meaning and an ancient vision of the world. Chief among them, the clear distinction between noun and verb structures. Every noun had three genders (masculine, feminine, neuter), three numbers (singular, plural, dual), and a case system. Every verb had two voices (active and middle/passive), three persons, and three numbers, as well as finite forms (indicative, subjunctive, optative, imperative) and nonfinite (participle and infinitive).

Also, as discussed earlier in this book, grammatical tense was of lesser importance than the aspect of an action. Actions were expressed as they must have been conceived by the Indo-Europeans: what mattered was how, not when, as well as the effects an action had on those speaking. Thus, the three verb tenses (present, aorist, perfect) indicated a verb's aspect, not its tense.

By a weird and spectacular accident of history, in the first millennium BC, ancient Greek appears to have already been fully formed, adult, present; nothing of its recent or distant past remained. In fact, none of the other languages that grew out of Proto-Indo-European emerge on the scene of recorded history quite like ancient Greek, with all its innovations and not a trace of how it had evolved. This is the Greek language's first step on a path unique to other Indo-European languages, a solitary path that would eventually become the one main road, as the history of the Greek language goes on to prove. It is the one language in Europe that continued to change from within and never turned into something other than itself.

Thus, the solitude of the Greek language; always.

Various Dialects and One Classical Greek: Yes, but Which One?

Greek turns up in history—and therefore before our eyes and in our books—in various guises. And how various! Every region and city had its own variations: the one we can read in official documents and the one we can read in private texts. Every literary genre has a canonical language, and every writer uses it to suit their own style.

Meaning that, between the sixth and fifth century BC, during the most ancient period of ancient Greek, there

were as many forms of Greek as there were texts (and just
think of all the varieties of the language as it was spoken!).
These varieties of ancient Greek are assembled into linguistic groups called dialects.

To grasp what understanding Greek and making oneself understood in Greek entailed, we must not lose sight
of the fact that the Greeks were never a unified state. But
they were a united, cohesive, proud *people*—and probably
always will be.

There never was such a thing as a Greek political state
(or rather, apart from periods of foreign rule, not until the
year 1832 AD). But a Greek people, that Greekness (τὸ
Ἑλληνικόν) described by Herodotus, has existed since the
time of Homer. Listen to how the Athenians assuage the
Spartans' fears that they might form an alliance with the
King of Persia:

Τὸ μὲν δεῖσαι Λακεδαιμονίους μὴ ὁμολογήσωμεν
τῷ βαρβάρῳ, κάρτα ἀνθρώπιον ἦν· ἀτὰρ αἰσχρῶς γε
οἴκατε ἐξεπιστάμενοι τὸ Ἀθηναίων φρόνημα ἀρρωδῆσαι,
ὅτι οὔτε χρυσός ἐστι γῆς οὐδαμόθι τοσοῦτος οὔτε χώρη
κάλλεϊ καὶ ἀρετῇ μέγα ὑπερφέρουσα, τὰ ἡμεῖς δεξάμενοι
ἐθέλοιμεν ἂν μηδίσαντες καταδουλῶσαι τὴν Ἑλλάδα.
Πολλά τε γὰρ καὶ μεγάλα ἐστὶ τὰ διακωλύοντα ταῦτα μὴ
ποιέειν μηδ' ἢν ἐθέλωμεν, πρῶτα μὲν καὶ μέγιστα τῶν
θεῶν τὰ ἀγάλματα καὶ τὰ οἰκήματα ἐμπεπρησμένα τε καὶ
συγκεχωσμένα, τοῖσι ἡμέας ἀναγκαίως ἔχει τιμωρέειν
ἐς τὰ μέγιστα μᾶλλον ἤ περ ὁμολογέειν τῷ ταῦτα
ἐργασαμένῳ, αὖτις δὲ τὸ Ἑλληνικὸν ἐὸν ὅμαιμόν τε καὶ
ὁμόγλωσσον καὶ θεῶν ἱδρύματά τε κοινὰ καὶ θυσίαι ἤθεά

τε ὁμότροπα, τῶν προδότας γενέσθαι Ἀθηναίους οὐκ ἂν εὖ ἔχοι.

It was most human that the Lacedaemonians should fear our making an agreement with the foreigner; but we think you do basely to be afraid, knowing the Athenian temper to be such that there is nowhere on earth such store of gold or such territory of surpassing fairness and excellence that the gift of it should win us to take the Persian part and enslave Hellas. For there are many great reasons why we should not do this, even if we so desired; first and chiefest, the burning and destruction of the adornments and temples of our gods, whom we are constrained to avenge to the uttermost rather than make covenants with the doer of these things, and next the kinship of all Greeks in blood and speech, and the shrines of gods and the sacrifices that we have in common, and the likeness of our way of life, to all which it would ill beseem Athenians to be false.[22]

That sense of Greekness is the one surprising yet fundamental detail for understanding the Greek language, be it prehistoric, classic, or modern. It is key to understanding Greek and to the intellectual pursuit at the heart of this book: to think like the Greeks and say so in their language.

The Greek polis, ἡ πόλις, originally stood for a strong

[22] Herodotus, *The Persian Wars*, Volume IV: Book 8, trans. A. D. Godley, Loeb Classical Library 120 (Cambridge, MA: Harvard University Press, 1925, 144).

military: a citadel or fortified town on par with the Roman *castrum* or German *Burg*. Its purpose was to defend the inhabitants against possible invaders or outsiders. It was typically located on high ground in order to dominate the skyline, which is why it was called an *acropolis*, ἡ ἀκρόπολις. Yet it wasn't long before the Greeks gathered inside the acropolis to build their most important places of worship, institutions, schools, and intellectual centers, making it the fulcrum of political and cultural power.

The word πόλις grew to mean the city—Athens, Sparta, Corinth, Thebes—and, for the Greeks, the word "city" meant home state. Occasionally a city would form federations and alliances with other cities, yet it would always jealously guard its traditions and values, as well as its particular language. A πόλις would never surrender its essence and reason for being: freedom. This union of people was based not on statutes, as Herodotus writes, but "the kinship of all Greeks in blood and speech, and the shrines of gods and the sacrifices that we have in common, and the likeness of our way of life." Moreover, Greeks from every region convened at the sanctuaries of Delphi and Olympia as well as at the Olympic Games. Absent any linguistic barrier, art, poetry, and philosophy spread far and wide, and intellectual debate took place throughout Magna Graecia.

Greekness (τὸ Ἑλληνικόνν) resisted Barbarism (βάρβαρος), a word used to describe any foreigner, near or far, whose language and culture differed from that of the Greeks.

Let's return to standard ancient Greek and its many dialects. We can say with confidence that during antiquity there was no spoken form of Greek that was autonomous and independent.

According to Thucydides, even before the Trojan War the Greeks somehow understood one another to be Hellenes, even though "as a whole [Greece] did not yet have this name." Οὐδὲ τοὔνομα τοῦτο ξύμπασά πω εἶχεν, writes the great historian in the "Archaeology," the opening of his study of the Peloponnesian War. *Archaeology*—as in the past. It was not until that mythic war that the Hellenes joined forces, fleets, armies, and a vision of the world to combat a common enemy, and finally rally around a single name.

The *Iliad* and the *Odyssey* may be the most important examples of a culturally and linguistically unified Greece. Written in an ad hoc literary language that merged Ionic Greek with various elements of dialect, Homer's poems about the Greek heroes' adventures in Troy became the most valuable source of words, styles, and idiom for the literature that followed, in every city and in every dialect. "From the beginning all learned from Homer," writes Xenophanes of Colophon, ἐξ ἀρχῆς καθ' Ὅμηρον, ἐπεὶ μεμαθήκασι πάντες. The *Iliad* and the *Odyssey* weren't just the poetic accounts of the Trojan War inspired by the abduction of Helen and Odysseus' return to Ithaca; they were an encyclopedia of Greekness. Through his hexameters, which singers traveled from town to town reciting by heart, men learned about the exploits of heroes and, more importantly, about what made them truly Greek. In fact, Homer sprinkles technical ideas throughout his poems: from catalogs of warships to observances of the dead, from divination to dietary habits, from ways of drinking wine to rules of hospitality, from cooking recipes to medical practices. There are even lessons in astronomy.

As Xenophanes tells us, all Greeks *learned* to fashion themselves as (authentically) Greek, to *differentiate* themselves, that is, from those for whom Greekness did not begin with Homer and the great breadth of social concepts (and social censure, naturally) contained in the *Iliad* and the *Odyssey*. These poems writ large were the ultimate guides to being Greek and to understanding what being Greek meant.

According to the historians, populations of Indo-European origin arrived in Greece at the start of the second millennium BC, during the time of the complex, advanced Mycenaean civilization. In 1953, the young Englishman Michael Ventris deciphered the clay tablets found in the Palace of Minos at Knossos, in Crete, and in other centers of power, including Pylos and Mycenae. The language on the tablets, which date back to 1450–1110 BC, is Mycenaean dialect, written in Linear B. This extraordinary discovery— made all the more important because, unlike the alphabetic script of classic Greek, the Mycenaeans adopted a syllabic script made up of 88 signs—enabled us to identify the main grammatical and lexical features of the most ancient Greek dialect ever to come down to us.

A second stage of Greek history is characterized by new waves of migration and events that are difficult to reconstruct. The so-called Greek Dark Ages abound with bleak legends concerning natural catastrophes: earthquakes, tsunamis, and sunken civilizations and islands. All of a sudden, writing disappeared. By the time it resurfaced, in the eighth century BC, the transformations of civilization and mass migration had ushered in a new language and culture, one that was utterly Greek.

Classical Greek is divided into five distinct dialect groups: Doric, Aeolic, Ionic-Attic, Arcadocypriot, and North Western Greek. Each variant mirrors the variety of Hellenic populations that combined to form Greece, the memory of which is consolidated in the epic, in poetry, and in the sagas.

The Dorians came from the northwest and settled in the Peloponnese. The Aeolians reached Thessaly, Boeotia, and the island of Lesbos. The Ionians were spread across Attica, the Cyclades, and Asia Minor. The other dialects are more complicated and harder to reconstruct. Arcadocypriot connects two geographically disparate areas: Arcadia in the Peloponnese, and Cyprus in the southern Mediterranean, not far from Turkey. North Western Greek, spoken in Delphi, Epirus, Argo, and Thebes, shares many attributes with the Doric dialect.

In addition to this extremely mottled, expressionistic portrait, there were the literary languages, dialectical varieties of every literary genre that were not determined by the author's language or place of origin, which they were free to use however they saw fit for the purposes of art and self-expression. Together with Aeolic, Ionic was the dialect of Homeric poems, poetry, and the lyric. The first instances of historiography, by Hecataeus of Miletus and Herodotus; of philosophy, by Heraclitus; and of medicine, by Hippocrates, emerged in the Ionic dialect of Asia Minor. But Attic, the πόλις par excellence of Athens, was the great and universal language of drama and prose, from Thucydides to Plato.

All of these varieties of Greek existed at the same time until the age of political unification and foreign rule under Alexander III of Macedon, when the language gave way and merged with Koine. That said, there was not a moment in Greek history when two Greeks were unable to communicate with one another.

So which Greek did people use to communicate with those who didn't live on the same little island or in the same small city-state? What was the lingua franca in Greece, a place as politically divided as it was geographically? And the last, most legitimate question of all may be: exactly which ancient Greek is it that we study today?

We must start by stating that the differences between one local dialect and another must have been marked—the dialect of Lesbos differed greatly from that of Sparta—yet not so different as to impede people from communicating with and understanding one another. That is because all Greek dialects are derived from that lost common Greek, of which they preserve every last essential feature.

Further, the differences between one dialect and another largely involved vowels; there were few major grammatical or lexical differences. To go out on a limb and make a contemporary comparison, far fewer differences existed between the Doric and Aeolic dialects than the number of differences that exist between the dialects spoken in Italy, like those between, say, Friulan and Tuscan. I could go a step further with my neat comparison and speculate that Greek dialects vary to the same degree as dialects spoken within the same region, say, in Italy, similar to the difference be-tween the Tuscan spoken in Florence and that spoken in Livorno. These differences are vast, yet the inhabitants of Pisa and Livorno are perfectly capable of understanding one another—if only they would bury the hatchet; their rivalry would make even an ancient Spartan quake in his sandals.

What is so extraordinary about ancient Greece is that it never imposed or established a common language through bureaucracy, literature, or religion. Nothing like their linguistic freedom and shared understanding exists in another language. Ancient Greek was always, therefore, a democratic language, in the truest sense of the word: Greek was vested in the people and their conception of the world, and they were totally free to exercise the language as they saw fit.

But what was the lingua franca for communicating? The language that birthed and instituted politics, philosophy, tragedy, comedy, science, and medicine? The language at the root of Greekness was the Attic of Athens, the πόλις par excellence.

The orator Isocrates leaves no room for doubt: Athens, thanks mainly to its culture, made Attic synonymous with Greek—Attic in its customs, in its literature, in its military alliances, in its funeral ceremonies.

Τοσοῦτον δ' ἀπολέλοιπεν ἡ πόλις ἡμῶν περὶ τὸ φρονεῖν καὶ λέγειν τοὺς ἄλλους ἀνθρώπους, ὥσθ' οἱ ταύτης μαθηταὶ τῶν ἄλλων διδάσκαλοι γεγόνασι, καὶ τὸ τῶν Ἑλλήνων ὄνομα πεποίηκε μηκέτι τοῦ γένους ἀλλὰ τῆς διανοίας δοκεῖν εἶναι, καὶ μᾶλλον Ἕλληνας καλεῖσθαι τοὺς τῆς παιδεύσεως τῆς ἡμετέρας ἢ τοὺς τῆς κοινῆς φύσεως μετέχοντας.

And so far has our city distanced the rest of mankind in thought and in speech that her pupils have become the teachers of the rest of the world; and she has brought it about that the name "Hellenes" suggests no longer a race but an intelligence, and that the title "Hellenes" is applied rather to those who share our culture than to those who share a common blood.[23]

If the language of Athens had achieved Koine status by the fifth century BC, and speaking Athenian automatically meant being Greek, that was not due to political power alone (otherwise, the rivalry between Athens and Sparta would have been cultural as well as political, and nothing of the sort really occurred). To return to Tuscany for a moment, standard Italian was not based on the Florentine dialect just because Florence was a great political power, but because Florence was the most prominent cultural center of Italy in the thirteenth century, home to the most important Renaissance writers and artists.

It was in Athens that Greek culture reached its peak—a peak humankind had never before reached. There, after centuries of study, architecture and the plastic arts attained perfection, drama took its definitive Panhellenic form, and

---

[23] Isocrates, *To Demonicus. To Nicocles. Nicocles or the Cyprians. Panegyricus. To Philip. Archidamus*, trans. George Norlin, Loeb Classical Library 209 (Cambridge, MA: Harvard University Press, 1928, 50).

philosophy and rhetoric were born. In short, the people of Athens dwelled in the essence of Greek thought every day. There, they breathed—and spoke—Greekness. For that reason, Ionic-Attic, the language of Athens, spread far and wide without having to resort to political pressure; the language didn't belong to the city but to all Greece.

Finally, to answer the most surprising question: Yes, the language studied today is almost exclusively the Greek of Athens. For centuries Ionic-Attic remained the most prominent Greek dialect, insofar as it was the means of expression for Aeschylus and Sophocles, Aristophanes and Thucydides, Plato and Isocrates, until Alexander the Great introduced Koine, which grew out of the immeasurable prestige of the Athenian language.

Κοινή διάλεκτος, or Greek After Classical Greek

Κοινή διάλεκτος refers to the language spoken in Greece, and understood wherever one spoke Greek, from the time of Alexander the Great.

Accounts of this next stage in the evolution of Greek are scant; mostly they come from inconsequential papyrus scrolls found in Egypt, as well as the New Testament, all of which is written in Koine Greek. But, as always in the extraordinary tale of the Greek language, we can track the before and after stages along this linguistic journey. Before Koine, there was the language of Athens, and after that, modern Greek. The latter almost exclusively grew out of Koine and not the ancient dialects—Ionic, Doric, Aeolic.

Taking that piece of information, we can once again em-
bark on the patient work of linguistic reconstruction by
looking at Koine. As well as at the transformations in Greek
society, of course.

At its outset, Greek life was not global in nature; every
kind of πόλις was its own small, independent, autonomous,
free state. The rugged, mountainous terrain of mainland
Greece was mostly isolated farmland. The colonies were
also isolated and almost always founded on islands or along
the coast—never inland.

When the Alexandrian empire came to power, every
πόλις lost its freedom, and therefore its reason for being.
Politics became the purview of sovereigns and their courts,
who governed Greece from afar. Economics, religion, bureaucracy, and commerce dwarfed the original islands and
regions to an extent no Greek person could fathom. At the
start of the Hellenistic Age, everything suddenly became
international and globalized, as the world understood those
terms back then.

In the Classical period, every person found the meaning
of their Greekness within the walls of their πόλις: in their
religious practices, culture, and traditions. Being human
was inextricable from being a citizen.

Though cities conserved their ceremonies and traditions
during Hellenism, these faded into mere holidays and rec-
reation. The Greeks came into contact with other religions,
and Greek deities were conflated with other deities in a
manner previously unthinkable. Moreover, being human
became equated with being a subject of a vast empire.

As a consequence, the Greeks were forced to move for

business and trade, traveling not only outside their πόλις but outside Greece proper. Soldiers who once served their homeland became mercenaries. Scientists and philosophers grew culturally isolated, no longer sharing their ideas with all of Greece, instead debating amongst themselves within the confines of schools and libraries. It was a full-scale revolution for the Greek people and their perception of the world.

It was Alexander the Great's father, Phillip II, who stripped the Greek cities of their independence at the Battle of Chaeronea in 338 BC. After the defeat, Greece ceased to exist as a political state and would have to wait almost 2,000 years before regaining autonomy on the world map.

By the time Alexander died in 323 BC, having expanded the borders of his empire all the way to India, conquering Asia Minor, Persia, Babylonia, and Egypt along the way, Athens and other Greek cities were little more than out-posts, and its inhabitants pined for the past. Other seats of cultural power were erected with renewed intellectual vigor, often far from the Mediterranean Sea, where the essence of Greekness had been formed. Artists, politicians, and scien-tists operated in Alexandria, Antioch, and Pergamon. Yet despite being relegated to the outer edges, Hellenic culture prevailed in this new, upside-down universe.

In the fifth century BC, Greece was so prestigious that the Macedonian kings—whom the Greeks disparaged as barbarians—did all they could to "Hellenize" or "Atticize" themselves, seeing as Athens was the world's cultural standard bearer. Alexander I of Macedon, whose love of

Greece earned him the name "Philhellene," claimed he was a descendant of Heracles and was even allowed to compete in the Olympic Games, where he dedicated a statue to himself in Delphi. The poet Euripides and the painter Zeuxis were invited to stay at the court of King Archelaus. All Macedonian nobles had Greek names, and Phillip spoke and wrote in fluent Athenian. As if that weren't enough, Alexander the Great was tutored by Aristotle!

This explains why we don't possess a sentence of Macedonian and know nothing of the country's language; the language of the Macedonian court had been Classical Greek for a long time. Greece may have been politically conquered by Macedonia in the fourth century, but Macedonia had let itself to be culturally conquered by Greece at least a century before.

The common language of the Hellenistic period, Koine was largely based on the language of Athens, the Ionic-Attic that was already the common language of Greek culture. But a language born inside the walls of Athens, the expression of modest-sized Attica, could not withstand the impact of being spread over a territory that stretched from India to Egypt.

Koine is the language of an empire, an outcome of war and occupation. Still, for centuries, people from all over—Egyptians, Persians, Greeks, Syrians, Macedonians, Arabs, and Iranians—adopted Greek as the lingua franca, the institutionalized language for understanding one another and making oneself understood when conducting business. Yet none of these groups abandoned their own idiom, the expression of their civilization and their intimate way of life.

Koine may have been the dominant language, the unifying tool with which to silence demands for local autonomy, but it was also the language of culture, of the scholarly and literary tradition. And it is in this language that we read the works of Polybius, Plutarch, the Greek versions of the Bible—the Jews had taken refuge in Egypt then—and, therefore, the Gospels.

But what kind of culture could Hellenism produce? A language as generalist as Koine is doomed to lose a lot, including almost all of its poetry. By the Hellenistic period, Koine no longer possessed most of the unique qualities of Classical Greek, and poetry was largely an imitative form; people wrote in the language of Homer and Hesiod out of a feeling of inadequacy or in order to hang on to its memory, but they never grasped its intimacy. Koine, on the other hand, was a flexible, concise tool, perfect for science and philosophy. It is during this period that straightforward terms for expressing abstract concepts were invented, and simple words for expressing difficult ideas were found.

The common tongue during Hellenism exercised a sizeable influence over almost all European languages; to this day, we borrow Greek terms for expressing abstract ideas—even ideas foreign to ancient Greeks. The relatively recent creation of words like *telephone*, *microphone,* and *television*, words based on Hellenistic terms, attest to how Koine and its global spirit have extended to our own day.

Finally, the Hellenistic period is the age that gives us Christianity, and this new religion immediately chose to communicate its message in Koine. When Christianity spread beyond Rome and the Roman Empire, it brought with it all that it had inherited from the Greek language. Nearly every new word in the Christian religion, whether Latin, Coptic, or Armenian, bore traces of Hellenistic Greek.

A language like Koine, which no longer belongs to a particular region, nor to a particular people, yet is spoken by a vast number of foreigners, ends up losing the world view from which it arose. Just as Ionic-Attic changed each society that spoke it, so too did it change, slipping into a relentless process of banalization, its meaning and memory gone. The characteristics that Classical Greek inherited from Proto-Indo-European were too extraordinary to survive: the times demanded a simple, ordinary, regular language that could be understood by everyone.

The linguistic changes—or losses, forgotten parts, misunderstandings—ensued rapidly under the weight of the Hellenistic empire. The original quantitative rhythm of Greek disappeared and was replaced with the qualitative rhythm of modern Greek. The non-Greek peoples who used Koine every day could not distinguish long vowels from short—the numerous errors found in scrolls involving η/ε and ο/ω confirm as much. Dual number vanished, as it had from many Indo-European languages long before, and the optative mood to express desire was deemed superfluous and merged with the subjunctive. Every irregular (in other words, original) noun or verb was suppressed and normalized, because eccentric and therefore incomprehensible.

In this convulsive and complicated age, people were

driven by their frenetic need to know *when* and lost sight of the value of *how* life unfolds. The moment time became the dominant linguistic category, the category of verbal aspect fizzled out, like a candle that had burned too long.

In the age of Koine, Greek was still a living language, spoken everywhere by thousands if not millions of people. Yet Greek had been sapped of almost all of its original meaning. Taking our time, carefully considering the significance of a language, we must ask ourselves what was left of *ancient* Greek by the second century BC. What was left of the language of Plato, Sophocles, Euripides, and Homer? Of the language that we study today? What distinguishes a living language from a dead one?

If the Greeks themselves no longer comprehended ancient Greek two thousand years ago, how on earth can we expect to comprehend it now?

Writing this book, I came to realize that the rupture in meaning between ourselves and the Greeks lies there, in the age of Hellenism and Koine—not in the halls of a Classics department. Coincidently, what was forgotten during this period of Greek history was exactly what I sought to remember by writing this book. The moment the Greeks ceased to think like *ancient* Greeks, *ancient* Greek may have died. Or maybe it just began the dying process; never mind that the Greek verb θνήσκω, "to die," only takes the ancient present aspect.

What is clear is that when a language becomes everybody's, it automatically becomes nobody's.

Modern Greek, i.e., Ancient Greek

Despite its longevity, Imperial Rome had little effect on the Greek spoken in the Mediterranean. The Greeks and those non-native peoples who adopted Greek—and, therefore, Greek thoughts and attitudes—took too much pride in their cultural superiority to switch to Latin. And besides, even the Romans viewed Greek as a prestigious language, which they insisted on learning during long sojourns in Athens. (Deep down, Latin never stopped envying Greek.)

Rome only succeeded in imposing its language on races open to social change: the Welsh, Spanish, North Africans, and inhabitants of present-day regions of Romania then known as Roman Dacia. But in Greece, the Romans felt like apprentices, and the Greeks were not willing to make changes to their society, much less their vocabulary. However, Greek did die out in Sicily and Italy, in that part of the world where, without the social force of mighty Koine, Magna Graecia had reached no further inland than the coast.

If every language that comes into contact with other languages absorbs loanwords (just think of all the English words that have entered Italian, and vice versa), no language proved as intransigent, in this sense, as Greek. Greek vigorously resisted loanwords, and when it did, those words indicated typically Roman entities, like transliterations of objects foreign to the Greek world, like κεντυρία "centurion," or ταβέλλα "an edict."

But with the impending spread of Christianity, Greek was doomed to cede its authority as a language. When the new religion was first liberalized and later officially adopted by the Romans, Latin became the official language of the Church of the West. In the East, on the other hand, the people who had initially chosen Greek Koine undertook to translate the new creed into their own languages—Gothic, Slavic, Armenian, and Coptic—as expressions of their own civilizations.

In this context, as Latin entered the Middle Ages and became the dominant language of culture and religion, Greek was confined to its own, increasingly narrow territory. Once again, the Greek language strayed from other languages, setting out on its own solitary path to arrive, via Byzantine Greek, at modern Greek.

During the Roman Empire, Greek intellectuals reacted to their decline by choosing the exact same solution they would adopt after the Greek War of Independence (1821–32), when modern Greece finally attained the political autonomy that it had sought for thousands of years. Their solution was unique: return, summarily, to the past.

A trend had in fact taken shape long before, with the Atticism of the second century BC, which would come to typify Greece's evolution—or lack thereof. To prevent losing their identity, the Greeks chose to resist the current, vulgar, *living* language then in use, in favor of its ancient, faded, *dead* forms, because they believed those forms conveyed the meaning of Greekness that they had mislaid. Greek intellectuals did everything in their power to memorialize even that part of the past that had been irretrievably lost. As a result, we find texts riddled with dual nouns, random syntactic and lexical embellishments, verbal anomalies that hadn't been seen since the days of Pericles, and long and short vowels deployed recklessly. Apparently, the Greeks didn't know how to respond to the changes taking place in society. They isolated themselves both politically and culturally, and the one aspect of their identity that they embraced was their shared past.

A combination of disquiet and nostalgia pervades all Greek history to the present day, and, from a linguistic point of view, leads to a purist tendency: a vain effort to keep the language from evolving, from drifting away from a glorious past, which may be too cumbersome to bear.

By the Byzantine age, a written language had been created that would forever be estranged from the spoken language, given that the latter, like all languages, continued to grow alongside the human beings who spoke it. Preventing people and languages from changing is impossible. But it is possible to ignore those changes, and that is exactly what Greek society did for more than a thousand years. The same Greek-turned-Byzantine was taught in every school, written in every book and every official document, and spoken by every sophisticated member of intellectual circles.

Local dialects, on the other hand, were gradually exiled to the countryside, far from the cities, and many variants that continue to exist in Greece date back to this period.

When the Turks seized control of Greece in the fifteenth century, the one cultural center left was Byzantium, where the Church had fashioned itself as the custodian of ancient Koine, the language in which Christianity was written and read. But the Eastern Roman Empire had slowly collapsed under the weight of foreign invasions.

Greater Greece had nothing to cling to but the sea, θάλαττα, as well as its ancient tongue, the one surviving relic of a civilization that by then lay in ruins; the language that the Greeks, instead of allowing it to evolve, tirelessly fought to preserve.

People's awareness of Greek civilization and identity came away gravely damaged after the decline of the Byzantine Empire and Ottoman rule. "Hellene," the appellation that defined the Greek people, had been abandoned: because Byzantium was part of the Roman Empire, the Greeks had taken to calling themselves Romans, Ῥωμαίοι.

At the turn of the nineteenth century, as Ottoman rule waned and Greece regained a sense of its own identity, the language situation was, to put it mildly, paradoxical. The traditional written language had remained largely faithful to ancient Athenian-based Koine, yet it was so removed from the language then spoken that people no longer understood it. And there was no one cultural, political, or social identity strong enough to impose its language on the new Greek society. The only center to safeguard Greekness over the centuries had been the Church, which had done so by conserving ancient Koine. So, people looked to it to provide the revival of Hellenism with a common language.

When the Greek War of Independence came to an end, the one way to recover a common outlook was to take a step back in time—two thousand years back. In fact, in its infancy, modern Greece established its identity by returning to its roots in Pericles' Athens of fifth century BC. Therefore, the written language that originated from Hellenistic Koine, which itself originated from the Ionic-Attic dialect, gave

Greece a united language that corresponded to their reac-
quired sense of national unity.

Modern Greek pronunciation was achieved by keeping
what was common to the majority of Hellenes and elimi-
nating all local quirks. The vowel sounds of Koine remained
intact, as did its written form. Modern Greek phonetics is
the same as Hellenistic phonetics, though some consonants
are pronounced differently. Although the grammatical
forms that had disappeared thousands of years before, like
aspect, dual number, the optative, and the dative, could not
be resurrected, in many regards *modern* Greek remained
ancient. The current language continues to draw a distinction between the present and aorist, retaining all of that
distinction's semantic value, and still uses the accusative,
nominative, genitive, and vocative cases (though the plural
genitive is rarely used, and the nominative and vocative are
often mixed up).

Modern Greek made two surprising innovations. It
got rid of infinitive verbs—a feature it shares with the
languages of the Balkans—and invented a future tense by
paraphrasing the verb "to want": "I will judge" is expressed
as θα κρίνω, "I want to judge"—and therefore "will judge."

This "purist language," καθαρεύουσα, is so deep-seated
that it approaches the Attic idiom of Athens. No one spoke
it when it was first established, but schools, literature, newspapers, the State, bureaucrats, and politicians managed
to introduce it into everyday parlance, with occasionally
startling consequences. Today, on military bases, people
commonly refer to a soldier with a rifle as a τα όπλα, or hop-
lite—the term for a Greek foot soldier in fifth century BC!

Like no other language before it, Modern Greek underwent a process of becoming notably more archaic. Unlike Italian, French, Spanish, Portuguese, and Romanian, which grew out of Latin, Greek is the only European language that never evolved into anything other than itself. Instead, it reacted to history by frantically retreating into itself.

But artificial and intransigent languages, languages that resist change, always run the risk of not being understood by people or running counter to their sense of identity. This gave rise to a prevailing tendency among intellectuals to mine the concrete, living language of the people, a language that had not been worn thin by thousands of years of literature.

In recent years, Greece has faced economic and political challenges unparalleled in Europe, challenges to both its identity and social dignity, and it has done so in a language that, however extraordinary, is centuries—make that millennia—old. The real challenge today, not only as concerns the language, is to find the will to finally reconstruct a modern idiom that would enable all Greeks to understand one another and make themselves understood today, both within their borders and more importantly without.

In his collection of aphorisms on the unhappiness of being a (modern) Greek, Nikos Dimou writes, bitterly, "Any race believing itself to be descended from the ancient Greeks would be automatically unhappy. Unless it could either forget them or surpass them."

As a matter of fact, Greece now speaks a modern Greek that borrows heavily from ancient Greek; in doing so, it reaffirms its identity as the people with the most impressive cultural past in the West. Yet as a people, the Greeks seem incapable of getting out from under that past, and they are constantly fighting for a present that has thus far failed to arrive—the future, on the other hand, was invented only a few centuries ago, with the verb "to want," by which, maybe, hopefully, they mean "to demand."

BIBLIOGRAPHY

> I had melancholy thoughts . . .
> A strangeness in my mind,
> A feeling that I was not for that hour,
> Nor for that place.
> —WILLIAM WORDSWORTH, *The Prelude*

I have consulted dozens of texts in order to put down in black and white my insights, hang-ups, feelings, and stubbornly held opinions concerning the Greek language, which I have cultivated over fifteen years of vigorous debate and heated discussions between me, myself, and I.

Even today, the book done, I still don't have any answer: most of the works that I scrutinized take great pains to reiterate more or less the same things that have been repeated in libraries and university classrooms for centuries. The essays definitely confirmed what I already knew, but they didn't tell me much about what I didn't.

Maybe "the strangeness in my mind" really is to blame, or my special sixth sense for Greek: the fact is, today I *think* in ancient Greek.

Just as Professor Emeritus Maria Grazia Ciani taught me to, I take full responsibility for what I have written in this book. Where I have erred, omitted, misunderstood, or made up, I apologize—starting now.

Most of the texts that contributed to the writing of this book were actually about life, not Greek. Sometimes they weren't even books but music, places, paintings, human beings.

As for specialist knowledge, here is a list of the texts I consulted:

Aloni, Antonio, ed. *La lingua dei Greci*. Rome: Carocci, 2011.

Campanile, Enrico, Bernard Comrie, and Calvert Watkins, eds. *Introduzione alla lingua e alla cultura degli Indoeuropei*. Bologna: Il Mulino, 2010.

Chantraine, Pierre. *Morphologie historique du grec*. Paris: Klincksieck, 1947.

Dimou, Nikous. *On the Unhappiness of Being Greek*. Translated by David Connolly. Alresford, UK: Zero Books, 2012.

Fanciullo, Franco. *Introduzione alla linguistica storica*. Bologna: il Mulino, 2011.

Heilmann, Luigi. *Grammatica storica della lingua greca*. Turin: Sei, 1963.

Hoffmann, Otto, Albert Debrunner, and Anton Scherer. *Geschichte der griechischen Sprache*. Berlin: de Gruyter, 1969.

Isidore of Seville, *The Etymologies of Isidore of Seville*. Edited and translated by Stephen A. Barney, J.A. Beach, Oliver Berghorf, W.J. Lewis. Cambridge, UK: Cambridge University Press, 2009.

Lehmann, Winfred P. *Theoretical Bases of Indo-European Linguistics*. London: Routledge, 1993.

Michelazzo, Francesco. *Nuovi itinerari alla scoperta del greco antico. Le strutture fondamentali della lingua greca: fonetica, morfologia, sintassi, semantica, pragmatica*. Florence: Firenze University Press, 2007.

Palmer, Leonard R. *The Greek Language*. London: Faber & Faber, 1980.

Pieraccioni, Dino. *Morfologia storica della lingua greca*. Florence: D'Anna, 1975.

Pierini, Rachele, and Renzo Tosi. *Capire il greco*, Bologna: Patron, 2014.

Pisani, Vittorio. *Storia della lingua greca*. Turin: Sei, 1960.

Szemerényi, Oswald J.L. *Introduction to Indo-European Linguistics*, 4th ed. Oxford, UK: Clarendon Press, 1997.

Villar, Francisco. *Los indoeuropeos y los orígenes de Europa. Lenguaje e historia.* Madrid: Gredos, 1991.

Woolf, Virginia. "On Not Knowing Greek." In *The Common Reader*. Reprint, Boston: Mariner Books, 2002.

Finally, some women walk this earth with lipstick in their handbag. I don't wear lipstick, but for over a decade, I have traveled from city to city carrying a copy of Antoine Meillet's incomparable *Aperçu d'une histoire de la langue grecque*, published in France by Hachette in 1913 and the liberating source of inspiration that set everything in motion and made it all meaningful.

Acknowledgments

> Well you've done it again, Virginia
> Made another masterpiece while I was dreaming.
> How does it feel to feel like you?
> Brilliant sugar brilliant sugar brilliant sugar turn over.
> —THE NATIONAL, "You've done it again, Virginia"

This book is the result of my strangeness, and the love of a few people.

Three years after the book was first published in Italy, I have decided to rewrite the acknowledgments for this American edition, to find the courage to confront the smoke and mirrors of memory.

Now as then, my first thanks go to Maria Grazia Ciani, Professor Emeritus at the University of Padua, whose correspondence aided the writing of every single page. I am immensely grateful for her love, scruple, openness, and friendship; I promise never to betray myself and to continue studying Greek—most of all, in order to know myself. Three years on, I am renewing that vow.

I can never forget to thank the friend who listened to me and supported me every day, who taught me so much and never left me hanging. I owe you a lot. *Stiamo tra di noi*, Alberto Cattaneo, always. (Only you have the photos of that crazy summer and of me as I was writing this crazy, life-changing book.) I love you.

Πάθει Μάθος, writes Aeschylus, "Understanding comes from sorrow." Over the last few years, when things have been toughest, I have absorbed this motto so fully that it has become etched in me—and freed me of my rancor.

Thanks to all those who were and are no longer my friends, because you never forgave me for being happy. Thanks to those who hurt and abandoned me, thanks to those who told me this would be impossible, thanks to those who forced me to apologize for succeeding in doing what I have always wanted to do: write. Thanks to you I have learned a lot—especially who I'm not.

Three years doesn't seem like a lot in the span of a life, yet they are if you live your days in the aorist.

Thanks to the readers who have accompanied me. I thought by writing this book I would be giving up a part of myself; instead I have rediscovered myself a thousand times over.

From South America to France, from Spain to Korea, from Holland to Singapore, thanks for your eyes, which never ceased to beam with curiosity and passion when I told you about "my" Greek. I couldn't do it without you.

Lastly, two great little things:

Thanks to my legendary dog Carlo, whom I thanked in the original edition of *The Ingenious Language*, for accompanying me from city to city, with those big eyes of his that say, "I trust you." He's no longer with us. The last time I thanked him, it made a lot of people smile. When he passed away, I promised him that I would thank him in all my future books. *Ferox invictaque*, as Horace says—I am and will remain so.

The Greeks believed that unlike the souls of humans, the souls of dogs do not descend to Hades. Immediately after they die, they return to the doorway of their house and wait for their owner to make the last journey together. I'll be waiting by the door every day, Carlo, because you managed to make my life in Sarajevo permanent (as I had hoped years ago).

This book is dedicated to the city of Sarajevo.

I want to thank my husband Zijad—*hvala*. You are my pluperfect of ὁράω, because I had seen it then, but I hadn't known it.

A α	B β	Γ γ	Δ δ
άλφα	βήτα	γάμμα	δέλτα
alpha	beta	gamma	delta
a	b	g/y	d
[a]	[v]	[ɣ~ʝ/ŋ~ɲ]	[ð]
I ι	K κ	Λ λ	M μ
ιώτα	κάππα	λάμδα	μυ
iota	kappa	lambda	mu
i	k	l	m
[i/ʝ/ɲ]	[k~c]	[l]	[m]
P ρ	Σ σ/ς	T τ	Υ υ
ρώ	σίγμα	ταυ	ύψιλο
rho	sigma	tau	upsilion
r/rh	s	t	u/y
[r]	[s~z]	[t]	[i]

E ε	Z ζ	H η	Θ θ
ἐψιλον	ζήτα	ήτα	θήτα
epsilon	zeta	eta	theta
ē	z	ē	th
[e]	[z]	[i]	[θ]

N ν	Ξ ξ	O o	Π π
νυ	ξι	όμικρον	πι
nu	xi	omikron	pi
n	ks/x	o	p
[n]	[ks]	[o]	[p]

Φ φ	X χ	Ψ ψ	Ω ω
φι	χι	ψι	ωμέγα
phi	hi	psi	omega
ph	kh/ch	ps	ō
[f]	[x~ç]	[ps]	[o]